P9-CDE-761

WHEN THE CHILDREN MARCHED

The Birmingham Civil Rights Movement

Robert H. Mayer

Enslow Publishers, Inc.
40 Industrial Road
Box 398
Berkeley Heights, NJ 07922
USA

http://www.enslow.com

Acknowledgments

Thanks to Julie Nord and Sarah Dunn for their excellent editing of early drafts.

Thanks to Joel Nathan Rosen for his critical reading of several manuscript chapters.

*Thanks to the wonderful staff of Reeves Library at
Moravian College for the many ways they helped.*

To Jan

Library of Congress Cataloging-in-Publication Data:

Mayer, Robert H., 1950–
    When the children marched : the Birmingham civil rights movement / Robert H. Mayer.
      p. cm. — (Prime)
    Summary: "Discusses the Birmingham civil rights movement, the great leaders of the movement, and the role of the children who helped fight for equal rights and to end segregation in Birmingham"—Provided by publisher.
    Includes bibliographical references and index.
    Audience: Grades 4–6.
    ISBN-13: 978-0-7660-2930-9
    ISBN-10: 0-7660-2930-1
    1. African Americans—Civil rights—Alabama—Birmingham—History—20th century—Juvenile literature. 2. African American children—Alabama—Birmingham—History—20th century—Juvenile literature. 3. African American civil rights workers—Alabama—Birmingham—Biography—Juvenile literature. 4. Civil rights movements—Alabama—Birmingham—History—20th century—Juvenile literature. 5. Birmingham (Ala.)—Race relations—History—20th century—Juvenile literature. I. Title.
    F334.B69N4485 2008
    323.1196'073—dc22

                      2007025590

Printed in the United States of America

10 9 8 7 6 5 4 3 2 1

Illustration Credits: Associated Press, pp. 1, 35, 36, 40, 48, 49, 54, 56, 61, 69, 70, 76, 78, 84, 88, 97, 103, 112, 116, 118, 126, 130, 148, 150–151, 154, 156; © Bettmann/CORBIS, p. 104; Black Star/Alamy, p. 107; Enslow Publishers, Inc., pp. 16, 17; Library of Congress, pp. 10, 13, 21, 24, 26, 95, 128, 134; Time & Life Pictures/Getty Images, p. 6.

Cover Illustration: Associated Press

Cover: Birmingham police escort African-American children to jail on May 4, 1963.

Contents

Chapter 1:
"Blown Into History" 5

Chapter 2:
The Reverend Shuttlesworth Fights On 15

Chapter 3:
The Movement Begins 29

Chapter 4:
The Arrest of Dr. King 43

Chapter 5:
The Children March 59

Chapter 6:
"Fire Hoses on Those Black Girls" 73

Chapter 7:
The Children March On 93

Chapter 8:
A Settlement Is Reached 109

Chapter 9:
Violence and More Violence 123

Chapter 10:
"Don't Try to Stop Us" 141

Timeline 157

Chapter Notes 159

Glossary 172

Further Reading and Internet Addresses 173

Index 174

I knew in a second, [a] split second, that the only reason God saved me was to lead the fight.[1]

—The Reverend Fred Shuttlesworth

"BLOWN INTO HISTORY"

The blast echoed throughout the neighborhood. They had bombed the reverend's home on Christmas night. James Roberson, a young parishioner who lived across the street, felt the shock in his own bedroom: "I was home in bed. The explosion was so powerful, I thought the world was coming to an end."[2] When Roberson gaped at the house, he saw a terrifying sight. A pillar had been torn from under the roof and the dwelling leaned to the left. Roberson feared for the people inside. From the street below he heard screaming.

Until the bomb exploded, it had been a normal, relaxing evening for the family of the Reverend Fred L. Shuttlesworth. The reverend sat in his bed talking to a visitor. His wife Ruby

The Reverend Fred Shuttlesworth stands outside the wreckage of his house following an assassination attempt involving sixteen sticks of dynamite in 1956.

watched television with their daughters, Ricky and Carolyn, and a friend. Fred Junior was in the dining room admiring the new red football jersey he had gotten that morning for Christmas. He was later to recall, "When I saw all that dust and stuff in the air, I knew that somebody had actually tried to kill us."[3]

Neighbors and church members rushed to the defense of the Shuttlesworth family. Some brought pistols; others even brought shotguns. They were enraged. But the reverend believed deeply in nonviolence. When he spoke to the crowd that night he told them, "Put those guns up. That's not what we are about. We are going to love our enemies."[4] And Shuttlesworth had a lot of enemies.

Segregated Birmingham

It was Birmingham, Alabama, in 1956. Reverend Fred Shuttles-worth, an African-American minister and civil rights leader, had upset many in the white community by pushing to integrate the public buses in Birmingham as Dr. Martin Luther King, Jr., had recently done in Montgomery, Alabama. Shuttlesworth had been threatening to bring King's successful campaign to town. In the days after Christmas, members of the black community had planned to sit in the whites-only sections of Birmingham buses. They wanted to challenge the city laws that reserved the front seating area for whites and the back of the bus for blacks.

It was not just the buses that were segregated in the city. As one reporter who visited Birmingham said, "Whites and blacks still walk the same streets. But the streets, the water

Handling the Aftermath

The Reverend Fred Shuttlesworth discussed an incident that occurred right after the bombing of his home:

> When I got out there was a terrific crowd all around, and one little ruddy-faced policeman was cursing out a Negro and I saw the Negro had a switchblade knife in his hand and the blade was sticking out. He had the advantage on the policeman at that time. The policeman had been rough with him, trying to make him move and everybody was mad seeing that thing that had happened. The Negro said, "If you put your hand on me again, I'll cut your throat to death. You are the cause of this thing; you policemen call yourself God and are the ones who are the cause of it. You all are the Klan."
>
> The policeman was red and I just came up and patted the young fellow [the man with the switchblade] on the back and said, "What are you so mad about? I came out of this; God spared me and I'm not mad at all. I want you to shut your knife up and there won't be any trouble." . . . and the Negro shut up his knife and went on.[5]

supply and the sewer system are about the only public facilities they share. Ball parks and taxicabs are segregated. So are libraries."[6]

King called Birmingham "the most segregated city in America."[7] The Birmingham brand of Jim Crow laws, the name used for the American system of segregation that separated blacks and whites, was particularly ugly. Separate black and white facilities existed for everything including hospitals, schools, playgrounds, and cemeteries. From birth to death, life in Birmingham was segregated.

The people of Birmingham experienced segregation as a regular aspect of their daily activities. Ed Gardner, a long-time Birmingham resident and activist, described his life in this manner:

> You could go downtown there in one department [of a store] and spend a thousand dollars and go to the lunch counter and be put in jail. Or you could go uptown and get on the elevator that was marked White Only, and get put in jail. . . . And then the eating places . . . had two doors. They had to have a sign on there, Colored and White, and then the owner had to have a wall inside there seven feet high so the black and white couldn't see each other.[8]

Then there were the buses. James Roberson recalled a sign posted on buses that read: "Colored, do not sit beyond this board."[9] Roberson described this as "one of the most powerful pieces of wood in the city."[10] Blacks had to sit behind the sign. When more and more whites got on, blacks had to give up their seats toward the front as the sign was moved farther back.

The situation in town provoked curiosity in some. Larry Russell remembered that as a child he wondered about the taste of "white" water from a "white" drinking fountain. Was it different from "colored" water? One day he and a friend stayed in J. J. Newberry's, a local department store, until closing. They snuck a drink from the "white" fountain and discovered there was no difference between the two. He did

Jim Crow Laws

The name Jim Crow was probably first used in the 1830s when a white performer applied black cork to his face and played an insulting character he called Jim Crow. The label, soon applied to blacks in general, became one more term used throughout the country to stereotype and slur African Americans. Jim Crow went on to refer to the web of laws and customs that kept African Americans in a separated and unequal position.

Much of the South was segregated because of the Jim Crow laws. Here, a boy takes a drink from the drinking fountain labeled "Colored" in Halifax, North Carolina, in 1938.

observe the generous spray of the "white" fountain compared to the slow drip of the fountain he normally used. Defenders of segregation often claimed that it provided "separate but equal" services for blacks and whites. But in the Jim Crow South, the separate facilities for blacks and whites were never equal.

Myrna Carter, who also grew up in Birmingham, recalled an incident from her youth that left a troubled memory. She was in a department store and observed a white women opening a drawer to look at some hats. A black woman did the same. As Carter recalled, "The saleslady acted like she had committed a crime. She told her, 'You don't go in those drawers. You wait until I get to you.'"[11] African Americans experienced such indignity on a daily basis in Birmingham.

As the accounts by James Roberson, Larry Russell, and Myrna Carter demonstrate, children suffered the indignities of segregation along with their parents. It is no surprise then that young people became deeply involved in the national struggle for civil rights. In fact, they played a central role in that fight as it happened in Birmingham.

The attack on the Shuttlesworth family was not an isolated incident. White racists used terror as a weapon against the black community and anyone else who threatened the racial status quo. In the 1940s, the Ku Klux Klan regularly fire-bombed the homes of blacks who lived in College Hill, a "white" section of town. College Hill became known as "Dynamite Hill." Attacks did not stop with the assault on the Shuttlesworths. Between 1947 and 1965, there were around fifty bombings of black churches and homes in the city.

All of them went unsolved. No wonder many began to call the city "Bombingham."[12]

For a time, this terrorism was very effective. Under threat of such violence, many people feared that segregation in Birmingham was an unchangeable fixture. Shuttlesworth and the people who came to trust him, however, refused to accept the situation as it was. They were ready to stand up and create a new world, even though standing up had a dangerous price tag.

The Reverend Shuttlesworth Rides the Buses

The Ku Klux Klan thought they could scare Shuttlesworth into stopping the bus protest by dynamiting his home. The bomb did not deter the reverend, but it did affect others. At a meeting the next day, many who had previously been ready to sit in the white area of the buses expressed doubts. "We ought to stop and think this thing out,"[13] they told others at the gathering.

Shuttlesworth would not back down from his position. "There's nothing to think out," he told them. "We said we're going to ride and we ride. We do what we say for a change. If you are nervous, I'm not binding you. But I am going to ride."[14]

The next day, on December 26, 1956, around 150 members of the black community rode the buses of Birmingham, and they sat in the sections designated for whites. Twenty-one were arrested.

Though the segregation laws were not changed immediately, something more important happened. Birmingham had found a leader: the Reverend Fred Shuttlesworth. People

Despite the bombing of his home, the Reverend Fred Shuttlesworth continued to protest. He and several other blacks rode in so-called whites-only sections of Birmingham's buses.

were amazed at his resolve. Despite the threat to his life, the man would not back down. In fact, the attack served to fuel both his faith and determination. The reverend later reflected on how he felt while looking through the rubble of his dynamited home: "I knew in a second, [a] split second, that the only reason God saved me was to lead the fight."[15] Later he would recall that night and state, "And this is where I was blown into history."[16]

Doctor, the Lord knew I lived in a hard town, so he gave me a hard head.[1]

—The Reverend Fred Shuttlesworth

THE REVEREND SHUTTLESWORTH FIGHTS ON

The crowd's anger filled the church. The Shuttlesworth family had been viciously attacked and many that night wanted to strike out in revenge. When the reverend spoke at the mass rally he encouraged a different path. "Now I want everybody to be calm. It happened to me; it didn't happen to you. And if I'm not mad, I don't see why you should get mad. I don't want any violence."[2] Since the bombing of his home and the protest against segregated buses, Shuttlesworth had continued to fight the Jim Crow laws. Reaction to one such challenge enraged the flock that evening.

This time the assault was over school segregation. Shuttlesworth had sent a petition to the superintendent

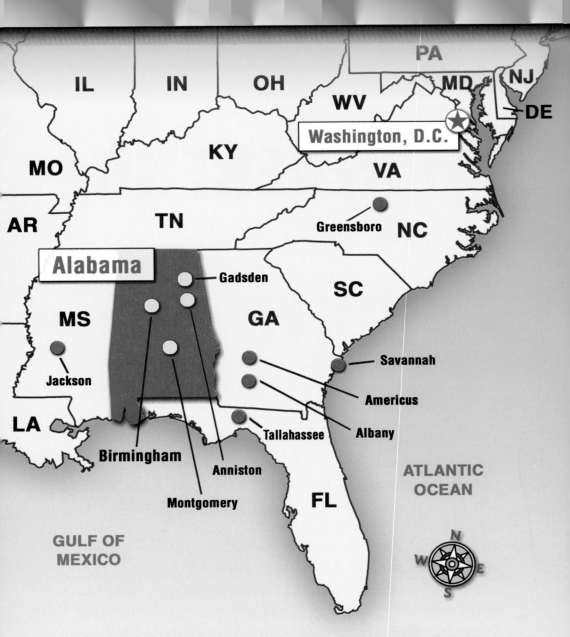

PA

IL   IN   OH   MD   NJ
            WV   DE
            Washington, D.C.
MO   KY
            VA
AR   TN   Greensboro   NC

Alabama   Gadsden
                SC
MS   GA
      Jackson   Savannah
                Americus
LA   Albany
      Birmingham   Tallahassee
            Anniston
         Montgomery   FL

ATLANTIC
OCEAN

GULF OF
MEXICO

N
W   E
S

The city of Birmingham, Alabama, and many other southern cities were involved in the civil rights movement of the 1950s and 1960s. At times, civil rights leaders traveled to Washington, D.C., to encourage reluctant politicians to support the movement.

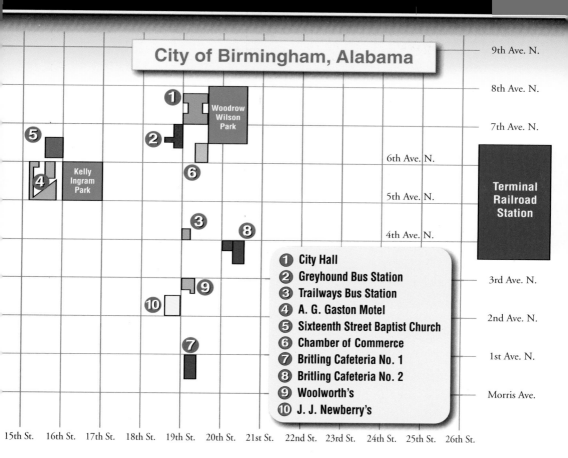

City of Birmingham, Alabama

1 City Hall
2 Greyhound Bus Station
3 Trailways Bus Station
4 A. G. Gaston Motel
5 Sixteenth Street Baptist Church
6 Chamber of Commerce
7 Britling Cafeteria No. 1
8 Britling Cafeteria No. 2
9 Woolworth's
10 J. J. Newberry's

Above are some of the places in Birmingham that played a part in the civil rights movement.

requesting that all-white Phillips High School be opened to nine black families. When the petition was ignored, Shuttlesworth took direct action. On the morning of September 9, 1957, he and his wife Ruby boarded a car with their two daughters, Pat and Ricky, and two young boys. They planned to enroll the four children at Phillips. Driven by the Reverend S. J. Phifer, the car made its way toward the high school.

No one knew what to expect. The reverend's daughter Ricky recalled: "I'm sure I was nervous the day we went, but then again I was with my father and that alleviated some of the nervousness. I didn't expect the mob that was there . . . I just thought, 'Are we going in there?'"[3] The swarm of fifteen to twenty white men must have been a terrifying sight. Shuttlesworth described them as "a mob of people armed with chains, brass knuckles, pipes and knives."[4]

Despite the hostile reception, the reverend got out of the car. Once out, he ran to avoid the attackers. His move was not successful:

> . . . I was beaten with a chain and brass knuckles, knocked several times to the ground, had most of the skin scrubbed off my face and ears, and was kicked in my face and side as members of the mob really set out to kill me. . . . As they did their gruesome but gleeful work on me, the whites shouted: "Kill this n_____ and it will be all over; don't let him get away; let's end it today."[5]

Meanwhile another group surrounded the car, pounding and smashing windows. Ruby Shuttlesworth got out to help her husband. Ricky started after her mom, but someone from the crowd slammed the door on her ankle. She got back in. Mrs. Shuttlesworth, seeing her children in danger, turned back to the car. It was not until later she realized that someone had stabbed her in the lower hip.

The reverend fought to get to the safety of his car. He knew that if he did not get back to the car, he would die right there on the street. And as Shuttlesworth lost consciousness, the others pulled him into the vehicle. Miraculously, they got to the hospital. The doctor who examined him wondered aloud why the reverend did not have a broken skull. Shuttlesworth explained, "Doctor, the Lord knew I lived in a hard town, so he gave me a hard head."[6]

The police arrested three men from the group of attackers. Despite the television coverage, newspaper photos, and clear identification by the reverend, the three were not indicted by the grand jury. Later, a reporter asked Shuttlesworth to explain the purpose for his civil rights activities. His vision guided his answer. Shuttlesworth told the reporters that he looked for a day when he could sit and talk in a friendly manner with his attackers. Though few clear-cut results were gained in this action, members of the African-American community in Birmingham were not deterred. They realized that it would take much more to end a system that had existed since the time of the Civil War and before.

The Birth of the Alabama Christian Movement for Human Rights

Shuttlesworth made sure that the years 1956 through 1963 would not be quiet ones in Birmingham. The governor of Alabama brought a legal end to the National Association for the Advancement of Colored People (NAACP) in the state of Alabama. Since the NAACP was the most important civil rights organization at the time, Shuttlesworth and his colleagues formed a new organization. It was called the Alabama Christian Movement for Human Rights (ACMHR).

The organization began at a mass rally held at Sardis Baptist Church in June of 1956. One thousand people attended. At the rally, Shuttlesworth defined the purpose of the ACMHR when he proclaimed: "Our citizens are restive under the dismal yoke of segregation. The Negro citizens of Birmingham are crying for leadership to better their condition. . . . The only thing we are interested in is uniting our people in seeing that the laws of the land are upheld according to the Constitution of the United States."[7]

The reverend believed that if segregation in the city was to be destroyed, it had to be fought on many fronts at the same time. For instance, several months before the Phillips High School incident, Fred and Ruby Shuttlesworth acted to desegregate the waiting rooms in the Birmingham train station. They strolled through the segregated waiting room, skirted a group of Ku Klux Klan members, and successfully boarded their bus to Atlanta. Minor successes such as this one buoyed the reverend's spirit.

Bringing African-American Police to the Force

The fight to include African-American policemen on the Birmingham force brought the reverend face-to-face with a man who was destined to be one of his great adversaries and a vicious enemy of the civil rights movement. The man's name was Theophilus Eugene "Bull" Connor. He was the newly elected commissioner of public safety as well as a secret member of the Ku Klux Klan. Shuttlesworth approached Connor and the other commissioners to request that they hire African-American police officers. In the midst of the reverend's request, Connor stopped him and queried, "Are you Shuttlesworth?"

"Yes sir, I am . . ."

The exchange went downhill from there, with the reverend continuing his petition and Bull Connor stating: "I think you have done more to set your people back and cause more trouble than any Negro ever in this town."

Shuttlesworth did not remain silent. "Mr. Commissioner . . . that's a matter for history to decide. The problem is what will *you* do?"

"I ain't doin' nothin' for you!"[8]

Needless to say, the request was denied.

Eugene "Bull" Conner would do his best to work against the Reverend Fred Shuttlesworth and the rest of those involved in the Birmingham civil rights movement.

When Connor went after Shuttlesworth, which he frequently did, the reverend never missed an opportunity to push right back. For instance, Connor was convinced that Shuttlesworth had bombed his own home on Christmas for publicity. Connor challenged the reverend to take a polygraph test to demonstrate his innocence. Shuttlesworth stated that he would do that if Commissioner Connor would also take a test to disprove charges that he was a member of the Klan and that he hated African Americans. Connor refused.

The Freedom Rides Come to Alabama

Just as Shuttlesworth and the ACMHR pressed for change within Birmingham, others fought for civil rights throughout the country. Events in the 1950s and 1960s merged into what historians would come to call the civil rights movement. Birmingham certainly felt all of the major developments in this movement including the Montgomery bus boycott, the drive to integrate schools, the lunch counter sit-ins and more.

The bus boycott, occurring southeast of Birmingham, provided inspiration across the country. The entire African-American community in Montgomery united to stay off the buses for a year, eventually winning a significant victory. In Greensboro, North Carolina, four young African-American college students sat in at a lunch counter not open to blacks and awakened the spirit of other young people ready to fight for change. One major civil rights event, the Freedom Rides, actually made its way into Birmingham.

The thirteen Freedom Riders, seven black and six white, boarded two buses in Washington, D.C., on May 4, 1961. The Riders wanted to force officials throughout the South to integrate interstate transportation facilities. When they stopped at stations, black riders would use waiting rooms, lunch counters, and bathrooms reserved for whites. White riders would use facilities for blacks. The Freedom Riders knew that such simple acts would likely provoke ugly and dangerous responses.

Little happened during the first days of the trip. As the Riders traveled through Alabama, events changed dramatically. On May 14, the two buses, one a Greyhound and the other a Trailways, left Atlanta. It was Mother's Day. When the Greyhound bus pulled into the terminal in Anniston, Alabama, a mob brandishing iron pipes surrounded the vehicle. They beat on the sides of the bus and slashed at the tires. The Riders wisely chose to stay on the bus and proceed to their next destination, Birmingham. A caravan of fifty cars followed them from the depot.

A tire went flat five miles out of town and the bus was forced to stop. The men from the cars stormed the bus and smashed windows. One from the mob lobbed a firebomb through a shattered window and others held the door shut. The passengers faced death. A state investigator on the bus forced the door open. As Riders fled the burning coach, they were beaten by the gang waiting for them outside. The Trailways bus, one hour behind them, was to meet a similar fate.

When the second bus arrived in Anniston, members of the crowd that had assaulted the first bus boarded the second. Freedom Riders were beaten and humiliated. The bus rolled on toward Birmingham and into a trap. In Birmingham, Klansmen filled the Trailways bus terminal. Bull Connor let it be known to the Klan that police would not arrive on the scene for fifteen minutes.[9] When the bus reached the Birmingham depot, the segregationists took advantage of this

Freedom Riders gather outside of their burning bus in Anniston, Alabama.

opportunity. As CBS news anchor Howard K. Smith, who was a witness, reported:

> They knocked some of the Riders to the ground, kicking, stomping, and beating them into bloody pulps. James Peck, one of the passengers, was struck with an iron pipe which opened his forehead and exposed his skull. The wound required 52 stitches to close, not to mention the cuts, bumps and bruises all over his body.[10]

Apparently, Bull Connor watched the slaughter from across the street.[11] Peck and other riders made it to the home of

Shuttlesworth, who saw to it that they received medical attention. The reverend also arranged a caravan of cars to rescue the first contingent of Freedom Riders, still in Anniston.

This chapter of the Freedom Rides ended when the Riders decided they would complete their trip by flying from Birmingham to New Orleans. Shuttlesworth thought that his job was done when he drove the group to the airport. He was wrong. Feeling that it was important to not let violence stop a movement goal, a group of students from a Nashville college came to Birmingham to complete the ride. They too experienced violent crowds. In fact, thousands of hostile whites surrounded a church in Montgomery where the Freedom Riders held a mass rally. Many of the riders were later arrested in Mississippi and spent time in the notorious jail known as Parchman Farm. Despite the resistance, the Freedom Riders accomplished their goals. In September 1962, the White House fulfilled an obligation from a Supreme Court case and put forth rulings that forbid segregation in interstate transportation facilities.

Thousands of hostile whites surrounded a church in Montgomery where the Freedom Riders held a mass rally.

Integrating the Parks

Shuttlesworth continued his push for integration. For many years, ACMHR brought lawsuits to integrate Birmingham's sixty-seven public parks, as well as other recreational facilities.

Shuttlesworth is booked on May 19, 1961, on two charges of conspiracy to incite a breach of the peace. During his fight for civil rights, he was often arrested.

All the parks in Birmingham were segregated, which meant that black people could not use facilities they supported with their taxes. After years of legal wrangling, Federal Judge H. H. Grooms ordered an end to segregation in city parks, playgrounds, swimming pools, and more by January 15, 1962. A significant victory for the reverend seemed likely. This was not to be. On January 1, 1962, Bull Connor and the city commissioners closed the city parks to everyone, black and white.

Much had occurred since 1956 when the Alabama Christian Movement for Human Rights had been founded, but not much had changed in Birmingham. As Shuttlesworth was to note some years later: "Negroes were 42 percent of its population and enjoyed zero percent of its privileges and opportunities."[12] Despite few concrete results, the fight for civil rights in Birmingham continued. The people in Birmingham must have found hope in the movement they saw growing throughout the South. New leaders such as Dr. Martin Luther King, Jr., had risen and new groups such as the Southern Christian Leadership Conference had arrived to push for change throughout the region. There was also a new leadership in the White House, which seemed, at times, ready to support civil rights efforts. In Birmingham itself, people were willing to keep fighting for justice despite what sometimes seemed to be a hopeless uphill climb. Dr. Martin Luther King, Jr., observed the determined leadership of the Reverend Fred Shuttlesworth matched by the doggedness of his followers and wondered if it was time to bring the eyes of the nation to Birmingham.

I said, "Well, on your slogan at the airport and elsewhere, 'It's so Nice to Have You in Birmingham' . . . we think that means King, too. We think he's nice enough to come in here."[1]

—The Reverend Fred Shuttlesworth to white businessmen who wanted to keep Martin Luther King, Jr., from demonstrating in Birmingham

THE MOVEMENT BEGINS

Shuttlesworth watched the troubling events taking place in Albany, Georgia. For nine months, from December 1961 to August 1962, nonviolent demonstrators attacked segregation in that small Georgia city. The activists tested segregation laws in the bus depot and marched against all forms of segregation in the town. They attempted to register African-American voters. The police arrested large numbers of protesters, mainly community members representing a wide range of ages and all walks of life. Dr. Martin Luther King, Jr., came to Albany, and he too was arrested. Despite the dedicated efforts of three civil rights organizations and the sacrifice of the community, not much changed.

Many people still argue over why there was little success in Albany. Some point to squabbling between King's organization, the Southern Christian Leadership Conference (SCLC), and the youthful Student Nonviolent Coordinating Committee (SNCC). These were the two groups running the efforts in Albany. Others suggest that the lack of clearly defined goals doomed the movement. The two groups tried to attack segregation on many fronts.

Some point to the "nonviolent" strategy used by Police Chief Laurie Prichett. He arrested demonstrators without being rough and treated them decently while in jail. Prichett charged them with violating local laws against segregation instead of national laws. As a result, less drama, limited publicity, and little involvement from the federal government took place. The entire experience must have been very discouraging for people in the civil rights struggle. The national movement for civil rights seemed to be sputtering, perhaps dying.

Planning the Birmingham Movement

When King and the leadership of the SCLC met in January 1963 to lick their wounds from Albany and plan their next move, Shuttlesworth stood up and spoke loudly. He observed that King and the SCLC needed a place to carry out their work and that the people of Birmingham needed national exposure to continue their fight against segregation. The reverend urged the SCLC to come to Birmingham and support the work he and others in the community had already begun. He told them, "Birmingham is where it's at, gentlemen. I assure you, if you come to Birmingham, we will not only gain prestige but really shake the country. If you win in Birmingham, as Birmingham goes, so goes the nation."[2]

King could not resist Shuttlesworth's invitation. The SCLC picked Birmingham as their next civil rights arena. With the lessons learned in Albany still fresh in their minds, the leaders began developing a strategy for the fight in Birmingham. They wondered: What muscle does the African-American community have with which to pressure the city of Birmingham? Only a minority of the African Americans had the right to vote, so they had little political power. Given that African Americans represented almost forty percent of the Birmingham population, the leadership of SCLC concluded that their greatest strength lay in economic power.

Here was the plan. The organizers would lead targeted demonstrations against certain downtown merchants. In support of the demonstrators, the black community would refuse to shop in white-owned department stores. In other words, they would stage an economic boycott. With Easter fast approaching, the boycott would cause the merchants to suffer without this seasonal business. The community traditionally bought new clothes for the holiday. But a question remained: Did the African-American community have the will to unite and fight a system that had been in place since the days of slavery? Shuttlesworth believed that they did, but only time would tell.

The Reverend Wyatt Tee Walker, executive director of the SCLC, was a thoughtful organizer who studied all parts of the proposed actions. He examined everything from the distances between the African-American churches and downtown stores to the number of stools at lunch counters. Walker studied the laws of Birmingham and estimated the amount needed to pay the bail of those arrested. After Albany, the SCLC proceeded with caution. Using all information he gathered, Walker generated a blueprint for toppling segregation in Birmingham, initially named Project X but later called Project C. (The C stood for confrontation.) Despite the careful planning, the protesters faced real danger. Bull Connor, who controlled the police in Birmingham, could be counted on to present the ugly and violent side of segregation. King ended that meeting on an ominous note, saying, "I want to make a point that I think everyone here should consider very carefully and decide if he wants to be with this campaign . . . I have to tell you in my judgment, some of the people sitting here today will not come back alive from this campaign. And I want you to think about it."[3]

> "Some of the people sitting here today will not come back alive from this campaign."
>
> —Dr. Martin Luther King, Jr.

Though the SCLC wanted to move forward, the protests had to wait. Birmingham was holding an election for mayor on March 5, and one of the candidates was Bull Connor himself. The leaders of the SCLC feared that demonstrations might cause some to vote for Connor, so they delayed their campaign. And when none of the three candidates won a majority, the city set up a second election for April 2 between the two top vote getters. They were Connor and a more moderate candidate,

Albert Boutwell. When Boutwell won that April election, Connor still did not step down. He challenged the vote in court. With Easter season fast approaching, the SCLC decided that they could wait no longer and moved forward.

There was one more delay for King. On March 27, 1963, Bernice Albertine was born to Martin Luther King, Jr., and his wife Coretta Scott King. As soon as Coretta Scott King and Bernice came home from the hospital, Martin Luther King, Jr., left for Birmingham.

The Marches Begin in Birmingham

King arrived during a sweltering period in Birmingham's history. According to local activist Ed Gardner, at the time of the marches ". . . didn't a drop of rain fall . . . It was hot and dry. Birmingham was hot."[4] Though the weather was searing, Dr. King's reception in Birmingham was somewhat cool. When Shuttlesworth met him at the Birmingham airport, King looked for his colleague, the Reverend J. L. Ware, head of the Baptist Ministers' Conference. Ware was not there, and that worried King. He needed the support of the African-American ministers and went immediately to a meeting of the conference. The ministers, however, did not welcome him. They apparently resented the idea of someone coming in from the outside to stir up trouble. Even after he spoke to them, they offered little support for the upcoming marches. King must have wondered whether Birmingham's African-American community was ready to unify around the protest. Despite the heat and the chilly reception, demonstrations started the very next day.

Before protests actually began, Lola Hendricks, an officer in the Alabama Christian Movement for Human Rights (ACMHR), went to Bull Connor informing him, "'. . . Commissioner Conner, we are here to ask for a permit to march downtown.' He said, 'I'll march you over to the city jail, that's where I'll march you.' I said, 'You're not going to give us a permit?' 'No I am not.' So I said thank you and we walked away."[5] Connor's refusal did not deter Shuttlesworth or King.

On Wednesday morning, April 3, 1963, sixty-five volunteers headed downtown and sought service at various eateries. At four of the establishments, the waitresses merely closed the counters and turned off the lights. At a fifth, the Britling Cafeteria, the police were called in and twenty-one people were arrested. The Klan showed up that day to confront demonstrators at the Woolworths lunch counter. One Klansman spit directly into the face of Calvin Woods, one of the demonstrators. Woods merely looked at the man and smiled.

Bull Connor was upset with the store owners who shut down. With the counters closed and owners not pressing charges, he could not arrest the demonstrators. As Connor stated, "If the merchants don't cooperate with the police, we can't move those Negroes out of their buildings."[6] He made his intentions clear to reporters when he told them that they could "rest assured that I will fill the jail if they violate the laws as long as I am at City Hall."[7] Connor's opponent in the recent election was no more supportive.

At a Thursday, April 4, press conference, King pronounced his satisfaction with the day's actions. He then asserted

The Reverend Fred Shuttlesworth speaks on April 4, 1963, in Birmingham as African Americans open a drive to end all segregation.

movement goals. The goals included the desegregation of lunch counters and other facilities in area stores, the active hiring of African-American clerks in department stores and elsewhere, the opening up of city parks so that all people could use them, the dropping of charges against those sitting in, and the creation of a biracial committee to study segregation practices in Birmingham.

That evening, five hundred supporters attended a mass rally at St. James Baptist Church. Such meetings were a regular fixture of the civil rights movement in Birmingham and became a nightly event during April and May. The gatherings

Black college student Dorothy Bell waits on April 4, 1963, at a downtown Birmingham whites-only lunch counter for service that never came. She was arrested with twenty others in sit-in attempts.

combined elements of a political rally with church services and included speeches, announcements, and the singing of both gospel and movement songs. At this particular rally, Shuttlesworth told the crowd his group had fought, "for seven long years and we don't intend to quit now. Twenty-five people came to me this morning and said, 'Here's my body.' I told them unless you are ready to go to jail and give your body and soul to our movement, then go home. What did they do? They went to jail."[8]

Dr. King also spoke. He reassured the people he would stay until the end and encouraged everyone to support the boycott against the downtown stores.

The Nonviolent Philosophy

People who marched that day practiced nonviolence. This was no accident. Dr. King, Shuttlesworth, and other movement leaders actively promoted a nonviolent philosophy to guide the movement. Marchers attended workshops to learn about the philosophy of nonviolence and to better understand why they were marching.

Leaders used sociodramas to train volunteers. As part of the sociodramas, individuals would play the part of violent and aggressive police officers or racist bystanders. Other volunteers would learn, as King stated, "to resist without bitterness; to be cursed and not reply; to be beaten and not hit back."[9] King made clear that nonviolence allowed activists to directly attack the system of segregation while working to change the hearts of individuals. Those who joined the movement signed a card that read: "I hereby pledge myself—my person and body—to the nonviolent movement." In signing the card, they agreed to "Refrain from the violence of fist, tongue, or heart."[10]

Though marchers practiced nonviolence, onlookers from within the African-American community did not always show such restraint. After years of living under a brutal system of segregation, many in the community seethed with great anger. While watching demonstrations and more police brutality, they expressed that anger.

When such rage was openly shown, activists approached those who seemed ready to strike back at authorities, calmed them down, and talked to them about the nonviolent philosophy behind the movement. They invited the angry individual to the nightly mass rallies so he or she could witness the spirit of the movement. At the rally, people from the movement would gather around the person as everyone sang freedom songs. They would then hear Dr. King speak and that would generally soothe the person's heart.

More Protests

The lunch counter sit-ins continued throughout the week. On Saturday, April 6, the demonstrators changed tactics. Instead of sitting in at lunch counters that could be closed, they marched. Shuttlesworth himself led the group of forty-five to City Hall. As he had told the crowd at the rally the night before, he planned to use the white water fountain in order to see if white water had a better taste than the water from the fountain marked colored. The group, wearing their Sunday best and carrying no signs, left from Kelly Ingram Park and marched down the street in pairs. The entire group had moved only three blocks when the police, along with Bull Connor, confronted them. "Let's get this thing over with," Connor told the police officers. "Call the wagons sergeant, I'm hungry."[11]

Through a bullhorn, the police gave three orders to disperse. In response, Shuttlesworth and his followers got down on their knees and prayed. The reverend asked the Lord to bless their actions, the city of Birmingham, and in particular, the police who were denying African Americans their rights. The Birmingham Police Department then arrested forty-two people, including Shuttlesworth. As the police loaded the arrested into vans that were so crowded the doors would not close, the marchers sang the movement's anthem, "We Shall Overcome."

On Sunday, April 7, Bull Connor brought out his police dogs. The Reverend A. D. King, Dr. King's brother, and two other robed ministers led thirty marchers to City Hall that Palm Sunday. Twenty-six were arrested while approximately a thousand people from the community looked on. When the marchers were taken into custody, angered observers on the fringes rushed toward the police vans. Police responded with their swinging clubs. Leroy Allen, one bystander, angered at the sight of billy clubs and dogs "slashed at one of the police dogs with a large knife."[12] The dog leapt on Allen, tearing his coat. Others in the crowd rushed to his aid. Movement leaders, fearing violence, spoke through a loudspeaker and urged the crowd to leave the streets and come into the churches. Many did and the demonstrations ended for the day.

The movement to end segregation in Birmingham did indeed continue, but it continued slowly. On Wednesday,

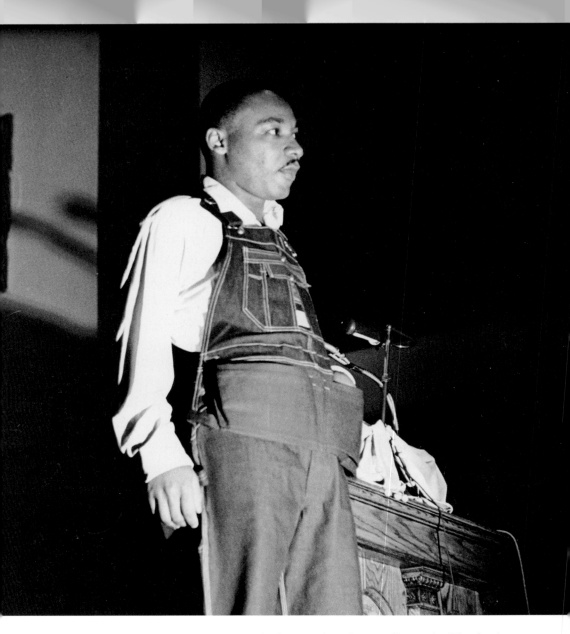

Martin Luther King, Jr., appears before a chanting audience in Birmingham, April 6, 1963. He proclaimed that all men should join him in wearing overalls until Easter as a demonstration against the segregation of city facilities.

April 10, there was a sit-in at the library, which was segregated like the rest of Birmingham. Eight black protesters roamed through the library, sat at desks, and read magazines while white patrons offered remarks such as "It stinks in here" and "Why don't you go home?"[13]

By that day, 150 people had been arrested. And though the community held marches, sit-ins, and other actions, the demonstrations lacked momentum. The SCLC could not find many volunteers ready to face jail. But even if there were to be mass arrests, the SCLC had few funds to pay bail bonds to get people out of jail. In addition, the national media generally ignored Birmingham. And as King's lieutenant, Andrew Young, stated, "In the white Birmingham community . . . and even in many black Birmingham churches and other established black circles, our campaign was being described as forced, ill-timed, and unnecessary."[14] President John F. Kennedy himself seemed to want no part of the Birmingham movement. Robert Kennedy, the attorney general and the president's brother, also called the demonstrations "ill-timed."[15] Some feared that Birmingham might become a failed action, like the recent demonstrations in Albany, Georgia. The movement to open up Birmingham clearly needed a spark. King and his close colleague, the Reverend Ralph Abernathy, would soon provide one.

One of the basic points in your statement is that the action that I and my associates have taken in Birmingham is untimely. . . . My friends, I must say to you that we have not made a single gain in civil rights without determined legal and nonviolent pressure.[1]

—Dr. Martin Luther King, Jr.,
Letter From Birmingham Jail

THE **ARREST** OF DR. KING

Bull Connor worked hard to stop the marching in Birmingham. He approached a state judge who was friendly with him, William A. Jenkins, Jr., and formally complained. Connor told the judge that demonstrations would "cause incidents of violence and bloodshed" and he hoped "to prevent irreparable injury to persons and property in the City of Birmingham."[2] In support of Connor, Jenkins issued an injunction, a judicial ruling. Jenkins ordered King, Shuttlesworth, and 133 others, to halt all forms of protests including "parading, demonstrating, boycotting, trespassing and picketing."[3] The stage was set for a historic confrontation.

While Connor schemed, King worked to counter the safety commissioner and energize the Birmingham movement. As he told people attending the mass rally on Wednesday, April 10, "Everyone in the movement must live a sacrificial life. . . . I can't think of a better day than Good Friday for a move for freedom."[4] The "move" he was referring to was his own arrest.

> "Everyone in the movement must live a sacrificial life."
>
> —Dr. Martin Luther King, Jr.

If King was to be arrested, he hoped to be joined by his colleague and close friend, the Reverend Ralph Abernathy. King and Abernathy first worked together during the days of the Montgomery Bus Boycott in 1955 and 1956. Afterward, they helped to form the Southern Christian Leadership Conference (SCLC), becoming president and vice president respectively. The Reverend Abernathy was right by King's side from the planning stages of the Birmingham movement through the days and nights of the marches.

After the Wednesday rally, King, Abernathy, and Shuttlesworth retired to the restaurant at the Gaston Motel. They drank coffee. It was 1:30 A.M. and now April 11, the day before Good Friday. The three talked casually, trying to ignore the reporters all around them. Everyone knew that something was up, so no one was surprised when Bull Connor's deputy entered at that early morning hour. He officially served the injunction to King as the reporters looked on.

Thursday night at a mass rally, Abernathy spoke and made their plans clear saying, "We are going to break the injunction that was issued and if they get another one, we will break it too. . . . We ain't afraid of white folks anymore. We are going to march tomorrow. We are going to a higher judge than Judge Jenkins."[5] It was becoming increasingly obvious that King and Abernathy planned to ignore the judge's ruling.

The Decision

Unfortunately for King, events quickly occurred that called his plans into question. The city informed the bondsman working to post bail for demonstrators that the SCLC did not have enough money to pay for all of their marchers. As a result, the bondsman could no longer pay to get protesters out of jail. King had to allow that if he was arrested, he would not be available to raise the money needed to free those who were or would be jailed. He felt a strong sense of responsibility to those people of Birmingham languishing in prison. On the other hand, he had promised to be arrested. King faced a dilemma.

On the morning of April 12, Good Friday, a group of twenty-five advisers met with King. Ed Gardner, a local African-American activist, described the scene this way: "Dr. King called a meeting at Room 30 at the Gaston Motel and said, 'Now, we got a court order here just served by the deputies that we can't march, but if we obey this order we are out of business. We got to violate it.'"[6] Tension drove the talk in the room. Everyone knew the consequences of the decision.

Older, more conservative members of the community urged caution. A. G. Gaston, local millionaire and owner of the Gaston Motel, and Lucius Pitts, president of Miles College, encouraged King to stay out of jail and to call off the marches in light of the injunction. Perhaps the greatest pressure came from King's own father, who was also a reverend. He urged his son to obey the injunction. Others strongly disagreed with those urging caution and the discussion got quite heated.

As the one who had to ultimately decide, Dr. Martin Luther King, Jr., listened with a critical ear. The Reverend Andrew Young portrayed the scene this way: "In this atmosphere of utter depression, Martin said very little. He lit a cigarette and just listened. . . . The arguments circled around the room ricocheting like a marble in a pinball machine."[7]

And what was Dr. King thinking? His account of those moments shows how deeply he reflected and all the factors he weighed:

> I sat there, conscious of twenty-four pairs of eyes. . . . I thought about the Birmingham Negroes already lining the streets of the city, waiting to see me put into practice what I had so passionately preached. How could my failure now to submit to arrest be explained to the local community? . . . Then my mind began to race in the opposite direction. Suppose I went to jail? What would happen to the three hundred [already in jail]? Where would the money come from to assure their release? . . . I was alone in that crowded room.[8]

Dr. King excused himself, went into the bedroom, closed the door, and contemplated his next move. He emerged thirty minutes later, wearing overalls and a workshirt, ready to be arrested. "'Gentlemen,' he said. 'Thank you for your words of advice, but we're going to have to march. Now.'"[9] The Reverend Ralph Abernathy, his close colleague, agreed to join him. The arguing in the room quickly evaporated as the twenty-five men and women joined hands and sang, "We Shall Overcome."

Dr. King Gets Arrested

At mid-afternoon, King, Abernathy, and fifty others exited from Zion Hill Baptist Church and walked down the sidewalk double file. They marched three blocks where they encountered a police barricade, and then they turned south toward downtown Birmingham. King remembered, "It was a beautiful march. . . . All along the way Negroes lined the streets. We were singing, and they were joining in. Occasionally the singing from the sidewalks was interspersed with bursts of applause."[10] The onlookers had grown so large in number, it was impossible to sort out the marchers from the spectators. The swelling crowds added to the atmosphere of excitement.

The police, surprised at the move south, quickly redeployed. The demonstrators turned east on Fifth Avenue and marched four-and-a-half blocks. There they met the redeployment and Bull Connor, who barked, "Stop them there."[11] The police grabbed the two ministers, threw them into waiting police vans, and hauled them off to jail. As Abernathy recalled, "Holding each of us by the seat of his pants, they propelled us toward a waiting paddywagon, lifted us in the air, and tossed us inside like a couple of sacks of meal."[12]

Dr. Martin Luther King, Jr., (front right) and Ralph Abernathy lead a column of demonstrators as they attempt to march to Birmingham city hall on April 12, 1963.

King (second from left) and Abernathy (right) are dragged toward a police patrol wagon to be taken to jail.

The other marchers lined up at the van and allowed themselves to be arrested.

The people gathered looked on in amazement. As Andrew Young described, "We were stunned by the aggressiveness of the police. . . . The crowd of bystanders became incensed, shouting, 'Don't rough up Dr. King, like that,' screaming at the police, and cursing them all."[13] A thousand from the community came out that day to observe the events and they ultimately became involved.

After overseeing the arrest of the fifty marchers, Connor turned next to the onlookers, ordering his men to move them off the streets. As the police advanced, they poked people with their nightsticks and frightened them with their dogs.

Emotions ran high and the "beautiful march" was about to turn into a riot. March organizers who had not been arrested wisely drew people into the nearby Sixteenth Street Baptist Church. Some men and boys remained in the park, hurling rocks and curses at police.

The next day the world experienced a newspaper picture of the two reverends being grabbed and heaved into the van.

Birmingham Jail

Meanwhile, Connor took Dr. Martin Luther King, Jr., and the Reverend Ralph Abernathy to the jailhouse, separated them from the other demonstrators, and placed them in solitary confinement. Being alone was particularly hard on Dr. King, an individual used to having many people around and lots of conversation.[14]

Here is how he spoke of that time in prison:

Those were the longest, most frustrating and bewildering hours I have lived. . . . You will never know the meaning of utter darkness until you have lain in such a dungeon, knowing that sunlight is streaming overhead and still seeing only darkness below.[15]

King sat in the cell completely alone throughout Good Friday and much of the day on Saturday, April 13.

Wyatt Tee Walker, SCLC's executive director, contacted the U.S. Justice Department and sent a telegram to the president urging him to intervene. There was no direct action from the president. Nonetheless, Bull Connor eased up, but only slightly. Late Saturday afternoon, King's lawyer came to the jail. The officer in charge told his guard: "Bring that nigger King down here."[16] King was reconnected with the world.

Two events occurred on Monday, April 15, that buoyed Dr. King's spirit. Coretta King had tried desperately to get in touch with her husband. She called President Kennedy. The president returned her call, reassuring Mrs. King that her husband was fine and that he would be calling her soon. The conversation between husband and wife took place later that day. The second event involved a meeting with a friend and movement lawyer, Clarence Jones. Jones reported to King that Harry Belafonte, the famous singer and activist, succeeded in raising fifty thousand dollars to be used for bail bonds. Jones's news provided huge relief for Dr. King. He had feared that by going to jail he would be unable to solicit funds for bail. Belafonte had taken care of that concern.

Dr. King's Message From Jail

Clarence Jones was also able to bring newspapers to King in jail. Much of the reporting troubled King, but one letter published in the Saturday *Birmingham News* troubled him the most. White clergy in Birmingham, who had tended to support integration, urged King to stop the demonstration. They wrote:

> However, we are now confronted by a series of demonstrations by some of our Negro citizens, directed and led in part by outsiders. . . . But we are convinced that these demonstrations are unwise and untimely. . . . Just as we formerly pointed out that 'hatred and violence have no sanction in our religious and political tradition,' we also point out that such actions as incite to hatred and violence, however technically peaceful those actions may be, have not contributed to the resolution of our local problems.[17]

King was both hurt and angered at his colleagues. He did not like that they called him an outsider and suggested that his actions incited violence and were "unwise." And he certainly did not agree that by waiting, Birmingham's African Americans would receive their rights. King began to compose his response around the margins of the newspapers brought in by Jones. The response was smuggled out, typed up, and brought back for final editing during later visits. His answer to the eight clergymen became known as "Letter from Birmingham Jail."

King addressed the accusation that the timing of the march was wrong and that blacks in Birmingham should wait:

> We know through painful experience that freedom is never voluntarily given by the oppressor; it must be

> demanded by the oppressed. Frankly, I have yet to engage in a direct-action campaign that was 'well timed' in the view of those who have not suffered unduly from the disease of segregation. For years now I have heard the word "Wait!" It rings in the ear of every Negro with piercing familiarity. This "Wait" has almost always meant "Never." We must come to see, with one of our distinguished jurists that, "justice too long delayed is justice denied."[18]

He then provided evidence that the injustice was so awful that it had to be confronted immediately:

> We have waited for more than 340 years for our constitutional and God-given rights. . . . Perhaps it is easy for those who have never felt the stinging darts of segregation to say "Wait." But when you have seen vicious mobs lynch your mothers and fathers at will and drown your sisters and brothers at whim; when you have seen hate-filled policemen curse, kick and even kill your black brothers and sisters; when you see the vast majority of your twenty million Negro brothers smothering in an airtight cage of poverty in the midst of an affluent society . . . when you take a cross-county drive and find it necessary to sleep night after night in the uncomfortable corners of your automobile because no motel will accept you; when you are humiliated day in and day out by nagging signs reading "white" and "colored" . . . when you are harried by day and haunted by night by the fact that you are a Negro, never quite knowing what to expect next, and are plagued with inner fears and outer resentments; when you are forever fighting a degenerating sense of "nobodiness"—then you will understand why we find it difficult to wait.[19]

Dr. King also responded to the charge that the SCLC represented "outsiders" to the Birmingham community by stating, "I was invited here. . . . But more basically, I am in

A handwritten copy of "Letter from Birmingham Jail" was displayed at the preview of a collection that was auctioned in New York City on June 21, 2006.

Birmingham because injustice is here. . . . I cannot sit idly by in Atlanta and not be concerned about what happens in Birmingham. Injustice anywhere is a threat to justice everywhere."[20]

The letter was also intellectually powerful. King tied the Birmingham movement to basic American, western, and Christian ideas:

Just as Socrates felt that it was necessary to create a tension in the mind so that individuals could rise from

the bondage of myths and half-truths to the unfettered realm of creative analysis and objective appraisal, so must we see the need for nonviolent gadflies to create the kind of tension in society that will help men rise from the dark depths of prejudice and racism to the majestic heights of understanding and brotherhood.[21]

In addition, King referred to Jesus, the apostle Paul, and the theologian St. Thomas Aquinas.

King explained why it was necessary to break laws. He discussed the idea of civil disobedience in this way: "I submit that an individual who breaks a law that conscience tells him is unjust, and who willingly accepts the penalty of imprisonment in order to arouse the conscience of the community over its injustice is in reality expressing the highest respect for law."[22]

King placed this view of civil disobedience in a historical context. "We should never forget that everything Adolph Hitler did in Germany was 'legal' and everything the freedom fighters did in Hungary was 'illegal.'"[23] As a dictator, Hitler made any laws he wanted; he often did this to persecute the Jews. In Hungary, people fought for their freedom from an oppressive Communist government, which made the laws.

Finally, Dr. King got even more passionate when addressing the clergymen whose letter led to his famous response. He accused them of being "more devoted to 'order' than to justice . . ."[24] and went on to wonder, "Is organized religion too inextricably bound to the status quo to save our nation and the world?"[25]

King's letter did not have much of an impact on what happened during April and May 1963. Newspapers and magazines were not quick to publish it. Today, however, it

Dr. Martin Luther King, Jr. (right), and the Reverend Ralph Abernathy are released from a Birmingham jail on April 20, 1963, after being there for eight days.

stands alongside the Federalist Papers and the Gettysburg Address as one of America's great documents. The statement is important because it conveys the meaning behind the Birmingham marches and the entire civil rights movement and in doing so helps to redefine American democracy.

The Ministers Released But What Next?

On Saturday, April 20, eight days after his arrest, King finally left jail. On Monday, April 21, the leaders of the march were tried for violating the injunction and found guilty. King was sentenced to five days in jail and a $50 fine. They were allowed to remain free while the sentence was appealed.

Despite all of the activity, there was genuine concern that things were slowing down. The national press was leaving town. The boycott of stores was apparently not too effective. Young, who did informal measures of the boycott's impact by going out to stores, saw many African-American shoppers. And the number of people willing to be arrested seemed to be dwindling. Wyatt Tee Walker put it this way: "We needed more troops. We had run out of troops. We had scraped the bottom of the barrel of adults who could go. . . . We needed something new."[26] There were hints of that "something new." On the day that King left jail, *The New York Times* reported more demonstrations and more arrests, but they could not give "a precise count . . . because several of those arrested were thought to be under 18 years of age."[27] The children were starting to march.

Kids, there's gonna be a party at the park. Bring your toothbrushes because lunch will be served.[1]

—Shelly "the Playboy" Stewart,
a Birmingham, Alabama,
disc jockey, using a code phrase
to announce the start of the
marches on May 2, 1963

THE CHILDREN MARCH

On the night of April 12, Dr. Martin Luther King, Jr.'s, arrest, Birmingham got its first taste of James Bevel. Bevel stood at the pulpit of the Sixteenth Street Baptist Church looking out at the crowd of three hundred. He expressed disappointment at the size of the gathering and quickly pronounced Birmingham as sick. Whites were sick because of their "blind hatred," and blacks were sick because they accepted their situation. After quoting Jesus's remark to a lame man, "rise, take up thy bed and walk," he proclaimed, "The Negro has been sitting here dead for three hundred years. It's time he got up and walked."[2] Police who were monitoring the meetings for Bull Connor claimed that Bevel "worked himself and the congregation into such a frenzie [sic] that we were unable to understand what he was saying."[3] That vehemence probably grew from Bevel's initial observation that the Birmingham movement was sputtering and perhaps dying. He took it as his duty to see that the campaign remained alive. Who was this man that seemed to appear on the scene from nowhere?

Even at first glance, it was clear that James Bevel was a bit unusual. For instance, he usually wore bib overalls, which made him stand out. And a yarmulke sat on his shaved head. This head covering, worn by observant Jews, seemed to be a strange article of clothing for a Christian minister. He wore it because he felt that Judaism and Christianity were intimately intertwined. The yarmulke also allowed him to feel connected with the ancient Hebrew prophets.

Wyatt Tee Walker called Bevel "one of the best tactical minds in our movement."[4] Others viewed him as simply eccentric. Clearly, he thought for himself and was unwilling to back down after making a decision.

From an early age, Bevel was a reader and an intellectual. He studied to become a minister at the American Baptist Theological Seminary in Nashville. There he participated in sit-ins at segregated lunch counters. That experience transformed him. He became deeply involved in the blossoming civil rights movement, joined the Southern Christian Leadership Conference (SCLC), and headed for Mississippi to help African Americans fight for the right to vote. That is where Bevel was when he received King's request for help. He jumped into his 1959 Rambler and drove to Birmingham.

The Reverend James Bevel often gave inspiring speeches in support of civil rights. Above, he speaks at a rally in Birmingham on May 9, 1963. At the right, he makes his case on August 14, 1962, at a church in Albany, Georgia.

Bevel Organizes the Young

On April 13, the day after his talk at the mass rally, Bevel began work that would transform the tone of the marches. He concluded that the best way to energize the movement was to recruit young people. As Bevel explained, here is how the SCLC mustered their young volunteers:

> We started organizing the prom queens of the high schools, the basketball stars, the football stars, to get the influence and power leaders involved. They in turn got all the other students involved. . . . They had a community they'd been in since elementary school, so they had bonded quite well.[5]

In addition, Bevel involved young adults such as Andrew Maririssett and James Orange to work with the kids. The student leaders listened to Bevel and others, returned to school, and spoke to fellow students.

Bevel found that the first to enlist were the young women. There are certainly many possible reasons for this, but Bevel felt that the philosophy of nonviolence was more "logical"[6] to young women than young men. Whatever the reason, women from the community came to play a central role in the marches.

Bevel's unusual approach took him first to two local disc jockeys, Shelly "the Playboy" Stewart and "Tall Paul" White. These men had what Bevel needed: a direct line to the young people in Birmingham's African-American community. They had a personal relationship with many of their fans, so when Stewart and White announced over the radio that a "hot luncheon" would be served at the Gaston Motel, listeners knew that this was a code to fool Bull Connor. The "hot luncheon" was really a planning meeting. Thirty student leaders from local high schools showed up for this strategy session with Bevel.

The message about education that Bevel delivered at the meeting probably went against everything these young people had heard throughout their lives. Parents told their kids, "Get an education and advance in life." Bevel told them:

> **You get an education in jail, too. In the schools you've been going to, they haven't taught you to be proud of yourselves . . . they haven't taught you the price of freedom. . . . The white man has brainwashed us. . . . We've got to start learning to love one another enough to say: as long as one Negro kid is in jail, we all want to be in jail. If everybody in town would be arrested, everybody will be free, wouldn't they?[7]**

As suggested by these words, James Bevel possessed a charisma that engaged the young people.

As a result of the recruitment effort, young people flocked to the workshops on nonviolence being held in the church basements. According to Andrew Young, one of the workshop organizers, the workshops provided "a quick, basic introduction to the philosophy and techniques of nonviolent protest. . . ."[8] Participants viewed films on nonviolent Indian leader Mohatma Ghandi, the Montgomery Bus Boycott, and the student sit-ins in Nashville. This gave the kids clear images of nonviolent protests. And James Bevel presented his lecture entitled "The Water Tower of Segregation." In it, he argued that "segregation could not last without psychological assistance from blacks themselves and a lack of faith in our own heritage and potential."[9] Bevel encouraged the young students to have pride in themselves and in their African-American roots.

Bevel was quite effective in attracting and energizing the young people. One story has it that he took some teens to a graveyard, pointed to gravestones and said, "In forty years you are going to be here. Now, what are you going to do while you're alive?"[10] Soon student attendance at the evening mass rallies created overflow crowds. The movement that had been fizzling only days before was coming to life.

As forcefully as Bevel went about his work, other adults in the movement criticized the idea of involving children in the marches. The more conservative leaders of the black community, such as millionaire A. G. Gaston, were shocked at the thought of including young people. Gaston stated, "As a responsible citizen of Birmingham, I deplore the invasion of our schools to enlist students for demonstrations during school hours."[11]

"School children participating in street demonstrations is a dangerous business."

—Attorney General Robert Kennedy

Also, from Washington, D.C., Robert Kennedy voiced a deeper concern: "School children participating in street demonstrations is a dangerous business. An injured, maimed or dead child is a price none of us can afford to pay."[12] The same fear must have been on the minds of every African-American parent in Birmingham.

A. G. Gaston

A. G. Gaston was a powerful force within Birmingham's African-American community. Gaston worked his way from being a millworker to a businessman, coming to own banks, real estate, funeral homes, and the Gaston Motel, where King stayed during the marches. In 1990, Gaston's businesses were worth $35 million. He was involved in the civil rights movement but tended to favor negotiations over marching.

Upon his release from jail, the Reverend King felt caught in the middle of the argument over whether or not to let young people march. While Gaston and others discouraged the inclusion of young people, Bevel, Andrew Young, and Fred Shuttlesworth pushed to involve the children. As Shuttlesworth said, "We got to use what we got."[13]

King faced the fact that during the early weeks of the movement not many adults had gone to jail. Even with the inspiration of his arrest, few had followed his lead. By the time of King's imprisonment, only three hundred Birmingham activists had gone to prison. On April 17, Andrew Young addressed a mass rally and called for volunteers. Only seven agreed to be arrested. King knew that for a nonviolent mass movement to succeed, the jails had to overflow. Many feared that the protests in Birmingham would die with no gains as the protests in Albany, Georgia, had failed the previous year. King listened carefully to both sides and, although the risks were great, he hesitantly agreed to let the children march.

The First Children's March

Bevel's young supporters leafleted the city's black high schools on Monday, April 29. The fliers they distributed called for walkouts at noon that Thursday. Bull Connor, hearing of the proposed action from the FBI, told the superintendent of schools to suspend any students who marched. If he kept young people out of the protests, he thought, the entire movement would just fall flat on its face. In one of his morning strategy meetings at a local bar, Connor asserted his hope that King would "run out of niggers."[14] When city hall turned down the Reverend Shuttlesworth's request for a parade permit, no one was surprised.

Eight hundred students throughout the city missed school that day.

Young people woke up on the hot Thursday morning of May 2 and turned on their radios. They heard Shelly the Playboy announce, "Kids, there's gonna be a party at the park. Bring your toothbrushes because lunch will be served."[15] Everyone went to school as usual, but at noon many left their classes and headed for the door. R. C. Johnson, principal of Parker High School, locked the front gates. This did not stop the students. They scaled the fences and headed to town. Eight hundred students throughout the city missed school that day.

The Sixteenth Street Baptist Church filled with young people ranging from the ages of six to eighteen. Each new contingent of students who arrived announced the name of their school as if they were at a pep rally. Cheers from other students met each announcement. Across the street, others from the community crammed into Kelly Ingram Park to witness the day's events. Birmingham police placed roadblocks on all the streets leading from the Sixteenth Street Baptist Church toward downtown.

At around one o'clock the first group of kids burst out of the church. They sang songs and carried signs as they headed for city hall. Many clapped their hands to provide a cadence for their marching step. When authorities approached that first group, the young people got down on their knees and prayed. The police quickly arrested them. The officers relaxed, thinking the demonstrations were over for the day. Bevel then sent the second group out. He kept the police off guard by releasing students in waves of ten to fifty. Though most marchers advanced only a few blocks, one ambitious group of twenty did make it to city hall.

As young people emerged from the church, one policeman asked Shuttlesworth, "How many more have you got?" He replied, "At least 1,000 more."[16]

Many of those who marched were even younger than the high school students. Audrey Faye Hendricks was nine at the time of the marches and described her involvement:

> I did not go to school the day I went on the march. I wasn't nervous or scared. We started from Sixteenth Street Church. We always sang when we left the church.

The singing was like a jubilance. It was a release. And it also gave you calmness and reassurance.

We went down a little side street by Kelly Ingram Park and marched about half a block. Then the police put us in paddy wagons, and we went to Juvenile Hall. There were lots of kids, but I think I may have been the youngest child in there.[17]

Audrey stayed in jail for seven days, sleeping with eleven other girls in a small room.

Police arrested group after group of the demonstrators. Early in the day, police vans were brought out to cart the children away. The vans were soon not enough. As the day progressed, school buses hauled the protesters off to jail. Birmingham police arrested five hundred young people that day.[18] That was more than the combination of all previous arrests since the start of the protest.

The overall mood of the day was upbeat. A *New York Times* reporter described the demonstration in this way: "There was no resistance to arrest by the laughing, singing, groups of youngsters . . . Most of the marchers fell to their knees and prayed as the police stopped them."[19] Spectators cheered on the young people. One older lady shouted out, "Sing, children, sing," as they marched down the street.[20]

Despite the positive spirit, one ominous sign appeared. As the students moved through town, they could not help but notice the firetrucks poised on the streets. With no fire in sight, they must have wondered what the powerful hoses were going to be used for. The sight of the trucks certainly created curiosity and concern in their thoughts. The upbeat atmosphere would not remain the next day.

A six-year-old black girl waits for a policeman to take her name before she is led away to a police truck in Birmingham on May 2, 1962. Over 450 children were arrested for protesting that day.

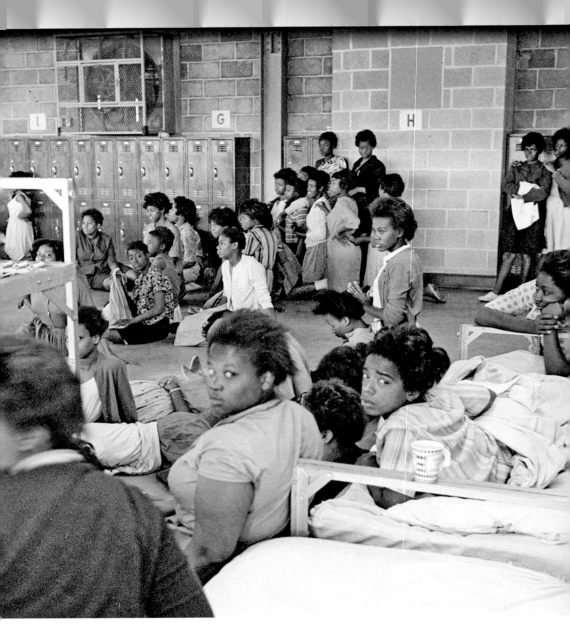

As the Birmingham jails filled with child and teen protesters, police had to find other places to house them. Here, African-American teenage girls sit in a room in the city hall on May 5, 1963.

Still at the mass meeting that night King proclaimed, "I have been inspired and moved today. I have never seen anything like it."[21]

Shuttlesworth announced, "The whole world is watching Birmingham tonight."[22]

James Bevel also stood at the pulpit and asked those inspired by what happened that day to raise their hands. "Now I want everybody that held up their hands to go to jail between now and Sunday because I want to be back in Mississippi . . . Tuesday."[23] Clearly, the children would continue to march.

But, lawyer Vann, they've turned fire hoses on those black girls. They're rolling that little girl there, right there in the middle of the street now. I can't talk anymore.[1]

—A. G. Gaston, as reported by David Vann

"FIRE HOSES ON THOSE BLACK GIRLS"

The marching children surprised and rattled Bull Connor. One Birmingham policeman observed, "You could see Bull moving, looking, concerned, fidgety. He was just desperate. 'What the hell do I do?'"[2] The police had arrested and jailed more than five hundred protesters on Thursday, May 2, 1963. Connor knew that he did not have much more space in his prison, which meant that Dr. Martin Luther King, Jr.'s campaign to fill the jails was succeeding. He needed a new strategy. Instead of locking up more demonstrators, Connor hatched a plot to brutalize the kids and frighten them off the streets.

While Connor schemed, the adults debated. Even after the impact of what was nicknamed "D-Day," many in the community still questioned the wisdom of letting the young march. During a morning planning session on Friday, May 3, A. G. Gaston demanded, "Let those kids stay in school. They don't know nothing." King gently responded, "Brother Gaston, let those people go into the streets where they'll learn something."[3] King prevailed. Given Connor's ominous plans and King's determination, the picnic mood of Thursday would turn ugly the next day.

On Friday morning students again heeded the call from local disc jockeys to attend the "party" in Kelly Ingram Park. Mary Gadson, a teenager at the time of the marches, describes her involvement this way: "I'd get to school and then go over the fence. We had listened to Shelley [disc jockey] on the radio that morning, so we knew what time to meet. Sometimes if the meeting was at ten o'clock, we would go to our first classes, and then be out for the rest of the day."[4]

> "If you take part in the marches today you are going to jail but for a good cause."
>
> —Dr. Martin Luther King, Jr.

At Parker High School one fourth of the students failed to show up that Friday. Instead, they again filled the Sixteenth Street Baptist Church, or they gathered in Kelly Ingram Park. Inside the church, King told the young people, "If you take part in the marches today you are going to jail but for a good cause."[5]

Outside in the park, anywhere from a thousand to fifteen hundred people crowded the square. People congregating in the park did not necessarily buy into the nonviolent philosophy preached within the walls of the churches. And throughout the area there were ominous signs. Fire trucks stood at several intersections around the park. Bull Connor, too, did not believe in the nonviolent approach, and a serious confrontation brewed.

At one o'clock the teens and young college students emerged from the church. The first groups served as decoys and headed west, away from the city. A larger group of sixty turned east, singing the word freedom to the tune of "Amen" as they moved forward. The young marchers had gone only two blocks when they encountered Connor, Police Captain G. V. Evans, and a group of firemen. Evans warned the kids to stop marching and disband "or you're going to get wet."[6] The young people ignored the warning and kept advancing.

The firemen turned a half-spray on the demonstrators causing some marchers to fall back and others to sit down on the pavement. Seeing the limited impact, the firemen then decided to use monitor guns in order to merge two streams into one. The surge of water gained in strength growing to a thrust of one hundred pounds. The water lifted some young people into the air, sent others sailing across the ground, and left some bleeding from injuries. The marchers, trained in nonviolence, took the blow. The front page of the Saturday, May 4, *The New York Times* carried a dramatic picture of teens being blasted by hoses while huddling in a doorway. People in the park and people standing on the roofs of nearby buildings felt outraged by what they saw.

Young African-American demonstrators sit on the sidewalk with hands behind their heads as high-pressure hoses are turned on their backs on May 3, 1963, in Birmingham.

Bull Connor Gets Even Tougher

Connor watched as his plan to intimidate young people instead of hauling them off to jail unraveled. More kids spilled out of the church. Police and firemen, distracted by the crowd in the park, could not stop the children's momentum. Groups made it to downtown where they were taken into custody.

The commissioner got even more desperate. First, Connor bolted the doors of the church and then he ordered, "Bring the dogs."[7] When Police Captain Evans gave the order to his men to "clear the park out" six German shepherds went to work.[8] Led through the crowd on taut leashes, dogs tore at arms, legs, and clothes. At least three people were bitten severely enough to seek treatment at a nearby hospital.

Here is Mary Gadson's description of the day's events:

> One demonstration I remember well. We were in a group that was supposed to march downtown, but we never made it because the police stopped us. Bull Connor was right out here on Sixth Avenue. He had the dogs out there, and he said if we marched, he was going to turn the dogs on us. They had the fire hoses also. That water was strong. It could knock you down. And he let 'em go and sprayed us. I got wet, and I almost got bitten. There were hundreds of us.[9]

Though Connor succeeded at arresting fewer that day, only 250 compared to 500 the previous day, he inflamed the crowd in and around Kelly Ingram Park. They booed the police and mocked the firemen. Then the firemen turned their hoses toward the crowd. The spectators continued to ridicule the firemen who in turn doused them with their hoses.

Above, African-American children stand behind a fence around the Birmingham jail after they were arrested. On the ground is a sign that reads "Justice for all, now!" Inset, a boy peers out from behind the fence.

The hosing persisted and intensified. Some moved to the roofs of buildings where they escalated their assault with rocks and bottles. King's nonviolent philosophy was threatened. Now, both the police and the march leaders feared there would be a riot. The two sides negotiated and the marches ended at three o'clock. James Bevel worked with the police, encouraging people to vacate Kelly Ingram Park. In the end, a major tragedy was averted, but barely. As stated in *The New York Times*, "There was an ugly overtone to the events today that was not present yesterday."[10]

Being Jailed in Birmingham

The jails were filled to capacity and overflowing by the end of Monday, May 6. This headline from *The New York Times* captured a sense of the crammed conditions: "Birmingham Jail Is So Crowded Breakfast Takes Four Hours."[11] The article explained that it took from 4:30 A.M. until 9 A.M. to provide everyone breakfast at the Birmingham city jail and the Southside jail. Officials told a reporter that the kids were being fed "as well or better than most of them have at home"; and the reporter noted, "The prisoners sleep on the floor almost shoulder-to-shoulder."[12] The jails were so filled that girls who were arrested were being kept at the 4-H club building on the Alabama State Fairgrounds land. Boys were held in the Jefferson County Jail and the Bessemer Jail.

Two girls discussed their jail experience:

Audrey Faye Hendricks:

> I was in jail seven days. We slept in little rooms with bunk beds. There were about twelve of us in a room. I was in a

room with my friends. We called ourselves Freedom Fighters, Freedom Riders. There were only one or two kids in jail who were delinquent. Everybody else was there because of the movement. We ate in a cafeteria. The food wasn't home cooking. I remember some grits, and they weren't too good. My parents could not get word to me for seven days.

We would get some news, like there was no more room in Juvenile Hall. They were taking the rest of the people to the fairgrounds because that was the only place to house them now. The jails were all full. I felt like I was helping to gain what we were trying to get, and that was freedom.[13]

Judy Tarver (seventeen at the time of the march):

Then they went to get school buses, and they hauled us to jail in Birmingham. . . .

Reverend King came by and he talked with us outside the fence. We felt better after that. We stood outside maybe two or three hours. Then they took us to juvenile detention by bus. By then it started to rain. We stood in the rain for a long time. I was in my white dress. Every senior girl started wearing white dresses the first of May, and wore them for a month until graduation. So there we were in our muddy white dresses.

Finally, we got inside. This must have been about eight or nine o'clock at night. We had left school at around one o'clock. They had prepared some peanut butter sandwiches and milk. This was the first thing we had eaten since noon.

The jails were full, so they loaded us on the bus again and took us to Fair Park. This was the same fairgrounds amusement park I couldn't go to as a kid because they didn't allow black people in there. It was pretty ironic.

They took us to the top floor of a two-story barracks building, which was nothing but a large empty room with mattresses on the floor. They had some policewomen

assigned to the girls. They searched everybody, and then told us to fall in.[14]

Response to the Children's March

Critics from all sides condemned King for using children in the marches. The recently elected mayor, Albert Boutwell, remarked, "When people who are not residents of this city, and who will not have to live with fearful consequences, come to the point of using innocent children as their tools . . . then the time has come for every responsible white and colored parent in this city to demand a halt."[15] And from another vantage, Malcolm X, the Nation of Islam leader, offered his view: "Real men don't put their children on the firing line."[16]

For the African-American community in Birmingham, the dogs and fire hoses represented a turning point. Though it was certainly not his intention, Bull Connor had succeeded in bringing the people together. Those who were initially not pleased with the presence of Martin Luther King, Jr., in their town were soon moved by the sight of local police and firemen assaulting their children. Nothing reflects this change more than the transformation of millionaire A. G. Gaston.

Gaston's conversion came while he watched the confrontation from his office window overlooking Kelly Ingram Park. White attorney and reformer David Vann described it this way:

> **Bull Connor brought the police dogs to the scene of the marches . . . and I remember I was talking to A. G. Gaston on the telephone, and he was expressing a great deal of resentment about King coming in and messing up the thing just when we were getting a new start, and then he said to me, "But lawyer Vann, they've turned**

fire hoses on those black girls. They're rolling that little girl there, right there in the middle of the street now. I can't talk anymore." And there in a twinkling of an eye, the whole black community was instantaneously consolidated behind King.[17]

At the mass rally held on the evening of Friday, May 3, at the Sixteenth Street Baptist Church, King addressed some important issues. With the rage and rock throwing fresh in their minds, leaders of the Southern Christian Leadership Conference (SCLC) wanted to reinforce the philosophy of nonviolence. Here is what King said: "Birmingham was a mean city today. But in spite of the meanness of Birmingham, we must confront her with our kindness and our goodness and our determination to be nonviolent. As difficult as it is, we must meet hate with love."[18] Andrew Young had earlier told them, "We have a nonviolent movement, but it's not nonviolent enough."[19] And King knew that many of the parents in the community were scared to have their children involved in the demonstrations. He tried to quell their fears with these remarks:

Now, finally, your children, your daughters and sons are in jail, many of them. And I'm sure many of the parents are here tonight. Don't worry about them. They are suffering for what they believe, and they are suffering to make the nation a better nation. . . . See, they're not there for being drunk. They're not in there for stealing chickens. They're not in there for embezzlement. They are political prisoners. . . . Don't worry about jail, for when you go to jail for a cause like this, the jails cease to be jails, they become havens for freedom and human dignity.[20]

A White Advocate

David Vann, a lawyer representing Birmingham's white population, negotiated with members of Birmingham's black community in April and May 1963. Vann later served as mayor of Birmingham from 1975–1979. As mayor, he proposed the construction of a museum commemorating the civil rights movement. The museum, the Birmingham Civil Rights Institute, stands today next to Kelly Ingram Park.

Throughout that talk, King made it clear to any who doubted it that the marching would continue, saying, "Now yesterday was a D-Day. And tomorrow will be a double D-Day." He told them, "And we're going on in spite of the dogs, in spite of the hoses, in spite of the tank. We can't stop now. We've gone to far to turn back."[21] When King spoke about demonstrating over the coming weekend, the crowd in the church cheered.

America Notices and the President Gets Involved

People throughout the world started to see the troubling images produced by events in Birmingham. The nightly news included footage of the battle in Kelly Ingram Park. And a famous picture of a young man being bitten by police dogs appeared on the front page of *The New York Times*, in *Time*

A seventeen-year-old member of the Birmingham community, not part of the demonstrations, is attacked by a police dog on May 3, 1963. This photo was published nationwide and made Americans take notice of what was happening in Birmingham.

magazine, and in other newspapers that week. Readers of the *Times* could gaze at the photo of a Birmingham policeman holding a dog leash in one hand and the young man's sweater in the other, while the dog dug his teeth into the victim's stomach. Birmingham was starting to be news.

In particular, Birmingham captured the attention of President John F. Kennedy. Throughout April and early May, Kennedy had said and done little about the events in Alabama. For instance, no one mentioned Birmingham at an April 24 press conference, but at a May 8 press conference, the topic dominated the conversation. With ugly images staring him directly in the eye, President Kennedy was hard pressed to ignore the dramatic marches.

On the afternoon of May 4, Kennedy was meeting with members of Americans for Democratic Action (ADA), a liberal political organization. He told participants how seeing the picture of the dog biting the young man made him "sick." Kennedy expressed anger over Birmingham: "I think it's terrible the picture in the paper. The fact of the matter that's just what Connor wants. And, as I say, Birmingham is the worst city in the South. They have done nothing for the Negroes in that community, so it is an intolerable situation, that there is no argument about."[22]

President Kennedy agreed when his brother Robert, the attorney general, sent Burke Marshall, Assistant Attorney General for Civil Rights, to Birmingham. Marshall's task was to nurture the limited negotiations that had already begun between the black and white communities. Arriving in Birmingham on Saturday, May 4, Marshall began the diplomatic process by meeting first with members of the Birmingham business community and then with SCLC. Marshall quickly discovered the truth of a sign hanging in his office that read, "Blessed are the peacemakers for they catch hell from both sides."[23]

Marshall weaved back and forth between the two communities. He arranged summits between small numbers of local blacks and whites, groups that rarely met. With the result from one conference, he would go speak with King, sometimes late into the night. Marshall worked hard to attain a wedge of agreement and then he would try to build from there. As Arthur Shores, a local African-American activist and lawyer, told a reporter: "He is here trying to bring about a meeting of minds between the two groups."[24] These behind-the-scenes negotiations took place while demonstrations continued.

The Protests Turn

On Saturday, Wyatt Tee Walker employed a new strategy. Around noon, demonstrators strolled into town in twos and threes and they carried no signs. Others carpooled into the boundaries of the city's white shopping district. As the duos and trios got close to City Hall, groups converged and one girl opened a banner that read, "Love God and thy neighbor." Bull Connor, coming from City Hall, saw the marchers and ordered their arrest. *The New York Times* reported, "Policemen marched them down a ramp into a detention pen in the basement of the big sandstone building. . . . They smiled at cameramen standing on the wall above them as the police led them away."[25]

Being unable to clearly identify protesters, Connor had his men detain any African Americans around city hall for fear they were part of the demonstrations. Another 127 were arrested that day. Connor successfully contained the demonstrations by having his police lock the doors of the two churches being used as staging grounds for the marches.

With those pledged to nonviolence trapped in the church, the streets were left for those less committed to the nonviolent philosophy driving the movement. Around three thousand people congregated in Kelly Ingram Park across form the Sixteenth Street Baptist Church, but the mood on the street got even worse than it had been the previous day.

The power of the water knocked people over and tore bark off the trees in the park.

Bull Connor, who had arrived on the scene from city hall, wanted to clear the park and again used the fire hoses. The power of the water knocked people over and tore bark off the trees in the park. Many left, but others stayed to taunt the police. Again, spectators stationed on rooftops hurled rocks and other projectiles at police. Wyatt Tee Walker described the scene in the park that day in this manner: "The blacks were waiting for something to happen; they started teasing the firemen; [the firemen] started putting water on them. It was a game. . . . They [the blacks] were trying to see who could stand up against the fire hoses. . . . It wasn't any damn battle; It was a Roman holiday."[26] And a young person who took part in the events confessed: "We thought it was fun."[27]

The Reverend James Bevel uses a policeman's megaphone to try to disperse a crowd of protesters that he thought could turn violent.

What appeared to be a festive atmosphere to some scared James Bevel. While wandering in the crowd, Bevel noticed twenty-five guns and several knives. He feared that violence might explode and lead to mayhem at any moment, so he asked the police for their bullhorn. Using his preacher voice, Bevel worked to quiet the crowd. Here is how he described his involvement that day:

> I took the bullhorn and I said, "Okay, get off the streets now, we're not going to have violence. If you're not going to respect policemen, you're not going to be in the movement." It's strange, I guess for them: I'm with the police talking through the bullhorn and giving orders and everybody was obeying the orders. It was like, wow. But what was at stake was the possibility of a riot.[28]

Bevel succeeded in quelling the disturbance. Overall, during the three days of the children's marches, eleven hundred had been arrested.[29]

The Miracle March

There was no lull in activity on Sunday, May 5. Much to the chagrin of Wyatt Tee Walker, Bevel challenged his authority and called off marches for that day. People still held a prayer meeting and rally at the New Pilgrim Baptist Church. Bevel, who had been part of the gathering, encouraged people to march inside the church. With spirits high, and again to the displeasure of Walker, at six o'clock Bevel led around fifteen hundred people out of the church on a "walk." "Let's not march. Let's walk,"[30] he told them.

The Reverend Charles Billups, a colleague of Fred Shuttlesworth's, replaced Bevel at the head of the line. Bevel was scheduled to lead marches the following day. The crowd, still dressed in their church clothes and singing "I want Jesus to walk with me," headed to Southside Jail in support of demonstrators being held there. Unlike previous demonstrations, young and old participated together in this march. Spectators, many sitting on porches along the parade route, were hushed.

The parade had walked about five blocks when they approached a barricade of policemen on motorcycles and firemen aiming their hoses. Bull Connor was there. Billups told the marchers to stop and to then get down on their knees and pray. He addressed the firemen directly proclaiming that the marchers would not turn back. Then he started chanting, "Turn on your water, turn loose your dogs, we will stand here till we die."[31] Others chanted with him. Myrna Carter, a teenage participant, recalled:

> And tears just started running down his [Reverend Billups] face. I'll never forget it. Bull Connor told the firemen, "Turn the water on! Turn the water on!" But they stood there frozen. "Turn the water on! Turn the water on!!" Then he started using profanity, cursing them, shaking the hose and shaking them. "Turn the hose on! Turn it on!" But those people just stood there. They would not turn the hoses on that Sunday. Then the whole group started singing Negro spirituals. It was just something in the air.[32]

Walker negotiated with Connor to let the people go to nearby Julius Eikberry Park to demonstrate. For thirty minutes they prayed in the park. They then headed back to the church, singing as they went.

Though some called the events that day a "miracle," the miraculous was explainable in more human terms. John Swindle, the fire chief and no fan of using fire hoses for crowd control, apparently "didn't hear" Connor's orders. Swindle's men "didn't hear" either.[33] This comment, overheard that day, seems to capture the spirit of most firemen present: "We're here to put out fires, not people."[34] But perhaps the most miraculous aspect of this event was the exuberance of the marchers. The adults discovered the spirit of their children and were now ready to march alongside them.

There are those who write history. There are those who make history. I don't know how many of you would be able to write a history book. But you are certainly making history, and you are experiencing history. And you will make it possible for the historians of the future to write a marvelous chapter.[1]

—Dr. Martin Luther King, Jr.,
May 6, 1963, Mass Rally
at St. Luke's Church,
Birmingham, Alabama

THE CHILDREN MARCH ON

On the "hot and muggy" morning of Monday, May 6, when the temperature rose to ninety degrees, the young people of Birmingham returned to center stage.[2] James Bevel made certain of that. He flooded the local African-American high schools with fliers that read: "Fight for freedom first then go to school. Join the thousands in jail who are making their witness for freedom. Come to the Sixteenth Street Baptist Church. . . . It's up to you to free our teachers, our parents, yourself and our country."[3]

Bevel's plea worked. Students roamed through the halls of Parker High School singing the word "freedom" and then filed out past the principal informing him, "Gotta GO,

Mister Johnson, gotta GO."[4] At one school, as reported in the *Birmingham News,* only 87 students out of 1,339 stuck around.[5] Instead, the students went to the church. Their playful manner suggested that the students did not realize just how momentous their actions would be that day. And this time the children did not march alone. The adults joined them.

Dick Gregory, a nightclub comedian and political activist, led the first march. Gregory related, "I arrived [in Birmingham] at 11:30 A.M. on a Monday, and an hour and a half later I went to jail with more than eight hundred other demonstrators."[6] Wearing a gray Italian suit and carrying a sign that said "Everybody wants freedom," Gregory ushered nineteen young people out of the church. They sang, "I ain't scared of your jail 'cause I want my freedom, want my freedom."

Police Captain George Wall, wearing a World War I helmet, confronted Gregory and asked him if he was leading the march. The comedian said he was. Wall then explained to him the laws they were violating by marching. "'Do you understand?' asked Captain Wall. "'No I don't'" replied the comedian. When Gregory refused to disperse, Wall first announced through the bullhorn, "Dick Gregrory says they will not disperse," and next, "Call the wagon."[7]

While some of Gregory's companions walked and others snake-danced into waiting police vans, two other groups of marchers bolted from the church. That was just the beginning. As *The New York Times* reported, ". . . and for the next hour, they kept coming in groups of 20, 30, 40 and 50."[8] King greeted the marchers as they left the church and urged

Civil Rights Comedian

Dick Gregory launched his career in standup comedy at a club in Chicago in 1961, eventually finding a national audience through television appearances. His satiric routines addressed social issues, especially issues involving race. Gregory used his stature to draw attention to the civil rights movement, often traveling to the South to march in support of various civil rights campaigns.

them to be nonviolent. "The world is watching you,"[9] he told them.

The crowds on the street cheered as the young people paraded, got arrested, and were driven off in police vehicles. Heading for jail, the kids continued to sing freedom songs as they beat out rhythms on the sides and floors of the buses. Meanwhile, Bull Connor, in his straw hat, egged the protesters on, saying, "All right, you-all send all them on over here. I got plenty of room in the jail."[10]

Waves of protesters emerged from the church. Police arrested some immediately, others after they kneeled on the sidewalk to pray, and still others as they reached the far end of Kelly Ingram Park. Some marchers started in the downtown areas. They too were immediately arrested. And though three red pumper trucks stood nearby, the hoses stayed dry.

The impact was overwhelming. Police hauled one thousand people off to jail that Monday.[11] The parents had decided they could no longer stand on the sidelines. Adults counted for half of those participating in the marches that day. With six hundred grown-ups taken to jail, the demonstrations truly became a multigenerational experience within the African-American community of Birmingham.[12] One historian stated that May 6 was "the largest single day of nonviolent arrests in American history."[13] After five weeks of demonstrations, Connor had arrested 2,425 marchers.[14] The jails were filled.

With thousands in attendance Monday evening, the mass rallies had to be held at four churches. Abernathy excited the crowd at one gathering with these words: "Day before

Three Folksingers
and a Reverend

Joan Baez, the white, northern folksinger, had attended the rally at New Pilgrim Baptist Church on Sunday and performed at Miles College that evening. On Monday, May 6, Baez snuck into the Sixteenth St. Baptist Church. To avoid arrest for integrating a black church, Baez snuck out of the sanctuary and back to the Gaston Motel where she was staying.

Overall, there was little white participation in the Birmingham marches. Northern folksingers Guy and Candie Carawan had been arrested marching on Sunday as was Barbara Deming, a reporter for *Nation* magazine. Probably the most significant white involvement came from the Reverend Joseph W. Ellwanger. He was a local, white Birmingham minister who was an active civil rights advocate. Ellwanger sat on the SCLC planning committee and helped to map out strategy.

Folk singer Joan Baez performs at the Newport Jazz Festival in Newport, Rhode Island, in 1963.

yesterday we filled up the jail. Today we filled up the jail yard. And tomorrow when they look up and see that number coming, I don't know what they are gonna do."[15] King made his rounds to each house of worship and delivered these dramatic words to the crowd at St. Luke's Church:

> I have never in my life had an experience like I am now having in Birmingham, Alabama. This is the most inspiring movement that has ever taken place in the United States of America. . . . There are those who write history, there are those who make history, there are those who experience history. I don't know how many historians we have in Birmingham tonight. I don't know how many of you would be able to write a history book. But you are certainly making history and you are experiencing history, and you will make it possible for the historians of the future to write a marvelous chapter.[16]

More Negotiating

As demonstrations shook Birmingham, negotiations continued. Burke Marshall met for two and a half hours in the morning with King. He tried to convince King to call off marches and wait until the new Boutwell government took over. Apparently, Marshall got nowhere with his pleas.

There were also meetings between more moderate whites such as Sidney Smyer, a local business leader, and attorney David Vann, and black leaders including Shuttlesworth, Andrew Young, Lucius Pitts, and A. G. Gaston. These negotiations also accomplished little. The black participants deemed potential compromises put forth by the white group as insufficient.

For once, the black community had the advantage and they intended to use it. The unity reflected in both the dramatic marches and the mammoth rallies that energized the people and gave them a true power. In addition, leaders in the movement began to notice another important consequence of the demonstrations. Citizens, both black and white, stayed away from the center of the city, creating a highly effective boycott of downtown businesses. Andrew Young noted, "not only had black customers stopped shopping, but the daily demonstrations, the omnipresent police cars and sirens, and the anxiety and tension surrounding the situation were also keeping white customers away from downtown Birmingham."[17] The boycott became a strong weapon in the fight to integrate and bring equality to Birmingham. With the power of their neighbors behind them, African-American negotiators fought even harder for movement demands.

Mounting Pressure

Bull Connor was getting increasingly desperate and determined. With the jails filled, he hoped to control events using force and fear, so he brought in reinforcements. Governor George Wallace supplied Connor with 250 Alabama highway patrolmen armed with submachine guns, sawed-off shotguns, and tear gas. More officers from the state came later in the week. Police from surrounding cities and civilians acting as a posse brought in by Dallas County Sheriff Jim Clark joined the law-enforcement officers.

Connor also employed an armored car that looked very much like a tank. The vehicle had six wheels and gun turrets.

An Unsympathetic Sheriff

Through his job as sheriff of Dallas County in Alabama, Jim Clark actively opposed any push for civil rights. The year after the Birmingham marches, he worked to thwart a voting rights campaign in Selma. Clark organized forces that beat activists attempting to march from Selma to Montgomery, Alabama, an event that became known as Bloody Sunday. Clark's brutality backfired and the U.S. Congress passed an important voting rights act in 1965.

As the vehicle roamed the streets on Tuesday, a voice from the loudspeaker on top demanded that people disperse. Hostile white crowds gathered near Kelly Ingram Park, though police barricades kept them back. Connor set the tone for the day telling a *New York Times* reporter, "We've just started to fight, if that's what they want. We were trying to be nice to them, but they won't let us be nice."[18]

Alabama Governor George Wallace started to become an ugly and threatening presence that hovered over Birmingham. The governor had made his views clear during his inaugural address back in January 1963 when he stated:

Today I have stood, where once Jefferson Davis stood, and took an oath to my people. It is very appropriate then that from this Cradle of the Confederacy, this very Heart of the Great Anglo-Saxon Southland, that today we sound the drum for freedom as have our generations of forebears before us done, time and time again through history. Let us rise to the call of freedom-loving blood that is in us and send our answer to the tyranny that clanks its chains upon the South. In the name of the greatest people that have ever trod this earth, I draw the line in the dust and toss the gauntlet before the feet of tyranny . . . *and I say . . . segregation today . . . segregation tomorrow . . . segregation forever.*

. . . But we warn those, of any group, who would follow the false doctrine of communistic amalgamation that we will not surrender our system of government . . . our freedom of race and religion . . . that freedom was won at a hard price and if it requires a hard price to retain it . . . we are able . . . and quite willing to pay it.[19]

The phrase "communistic amalgamation" was a reference to integration of blacks and whites. Wallace spoke as a determined segregationist and in stating his willingness to pay "a hard price" even suggested that he would use violence in opposing the civil rights movement.

Referring to events in Birmingham, Wallace told the Alabama state legislature on Tuesday, May 7, "I am beginning to tire of agitators, integrationists, and others who seek to destroy law and order in Alabama" and that he would "take whatever action I am called upon to take [to restore order]."[20] At the end of the day on Tuesday, Brigadier General Henry V. Graham, head of the Alabama National Guard, showed up in Birmingham, raising the possibility that martial law would be declared.

As the negotiations failed and as Connor and Wallace became even more threatening, the Student Nonviolent Coordinating Committee (SNCC) arrived on the scene. As the name would suggest, members of this civil rights organization tended to be younger than the leadership of Southern Christian Leadership Conference (SCLC) and more confrontational in their approach. In planning sessions that lasted all night on May 6, movement leaders from the SNCC and SCLC, including James Bevel, James Forman, and Dorothy Cotton, plotted a new strategy for the May 7 protest. Instead of the short march from the church leading to quick arrest and jailing, marchers would start in the downtown area with the intention of creating maximum chaos. The strategists aptly called the plan Operation Confusion. They hoped to sustain the boycott by disrupting downtown business and putting even more pressure on local businessmen. Given Connor, Wallace, and a steadfast African-American leadership, a classic and frightening confrontation threatened the day.

Tuesday Marches

Before the marches began on Tuesday, May 7, King appeared at a press conference where he announced, "Activities which have taken place in Birmingham over the last few days, to my mind, mark the nonviolent movement coming of age. This is the first time in the history of our struggle that we have been able, literally, to fill the jails."[21] Apparently, local Sheriff Melvin Bailey agreed when he confessed, "We've got a problem."[22] Only twenty-eight people were to be arrested in the course of the day's activities.[23] The jails were just too crowded.

The day's events happened like this. Bull Connor's police blocked all the streets that led downtown. Movement activities started at noon when small decoy groups left from the Sixteenth Street Baptist Church. This early starting time caught the police

Young African-American protesters cheer and applaud as they stand along a sidewalk in Birmingham on May 7, 1963, during an anti-segregation demonstration.

off guard as many were still at lunch. The children marched around the perimeter of the park and then returned to church. After one group came back, other children emerged. These maneuvers were a distraction for the real action. Also at noon, six hundred young demonstrators arranged in sixteen groups invaded downtown Birmingham from all directions. "Movement moms" and students from Miles College secretly drove into the city center and distributed signs from the trunks

Two young protesters in Birmingham try to avoid a jet of water from a fire hose on May 7, 1963.

of strategically parked cars.[24] As movement lawyer Len Holt described the scene: "The clock stuck noon. The students struck. Almost simultaneously, eight department stores were picketed."[25] Police tore up signs but made no arrests.

Meanwhile, back at the church, the door opened again and scores of protesters headed downtown in what Bevel called a "freedom dash."[26] Three thousand filled the streets, blocking traffic in the business district. As King described the scene:

> There were Negroes on the sidewalks, in the streets, standing, sitting in the aisles of downtown stores. There were square blocks of Negroes, a veritable sea of black faces. They were committing no violence; they were just present and singing. Downtown Birmingham echoed to the strains of the freedom songs.[27]

The momentum continued through the afternoon as Fred Shuttlesworth initiated a second march into the heart of the city.

And then at 2:45 a "riot" occurred at Kelly Ingram Park. At least that's what *The New York Times* called it. The violence started when black spectators "rained rocks, bottles and brickbats on the law-enforcement officials . . ."[28] With the massive police presence and the threatening words of Governor Wallace fresh in people's minds, the spiral of violence increased that afternoon. Fire hoses drove the people back. They quickly returned and again hurled stones at authorities. Police used their billy clubs liberally as they beat the onlookers in both nearby alleyways and within the park. Meanwhile, Bull Connor's armored car prowled the streets. Again, there were white crowds all around the park, but police barricades kept them back. This is what Len Holt, movement activist, experienced when he stepped out of the Sixteenth Street Baptist Church:

> When I emerged I saw 3,000 Negroes encircled in the Kelly-Ingram Park by policemen swinging clubs. The hoses were in action with the pressure wide open. On one side the students were confronted by clubs, on the other, powerful streams of water. The firemen used the hoses to knock down the students. As the streams hit trees, the bark was ripped off. Bricks were torn loose from the walls.[29]

Again, SCLC leaders urged the crowd to be nonviolent. A. D. King walked through the park with a police megaphone announcing, "You're not helping our cause."[30] King got little response. The struggle in Kelly Ingram Park lasted for an hour.[31]

Tuesday was also the day Birmingham authorities got even with Shuttlesworth. The reverend saw a kid in Kelly Ingram punch a cop and got worried that violence would escalate. While carrying a white flag, he led a group of three hundred young people who were in the park back to the Sixteenth Street Baptist Church. As he and the marchers went down an outside stairwell that lead to the church basement, he heard a fireman say, "Let's put some water on the reverend."[32] Shuttlesworth later recalled:

> I caught sight of the powerful stream of water arching down upon me from less than 50 feet away. Quickly I put my hands over my face and turned away as the water hurled me against the concrete. All breath was knocked out of me, my chest ached, my head pounded, and my heart was trying to burst. Had I not thrown up my hands, my face probably would have been disfigured today.[33]

Firemen use hoses to hit protesters with high-powered streams of water in Birmingham.

The pressure of the water slammed the reverend against the church wall. He went immediately to the hospital. Commissioner Connor told a reporter he was sorry that he was not present. "I waited a week to see Shuttlesworth get hit with a hose. I'm sorry I missed it." When informed that an ambulance had taken Shuttlesworth to the hospital, Connor stated, "I wish they'd carry him away in a hearse."[34] And in the midst of all the mayhem, negotiations continued.

The city of Birmingham has reached
an accord with its conscience.[1]

—Statement from African-American
leadership after settlement

A SETTLEMENT IS REACHED

With the threat of more demonstrations and increasing violence, Sidney Smyer observed the stalled negotiations between black and white partners. He sought a way to move the process forward. Smyer knew he needed the business community behind him for any agreement to hold. To garner that support, Smyer called upon the Senior Citizens Committee, seventy-seven of the most powerful white business leaders from Birmingham.[2] The committee was known less formally as the Big Mules. In the midst of the chaos, Smyer convened a meeting of the Mules in the chamber of commerce building downtown.

Burke Marshall was present with the business leaders on Tuesday, May 7, 1963. He must have been disappointed during the early parts of the meeting. Marshall heard one speaker call for a harsh form of martial law to stop the African-American protesters and another blame the Kennedy administration for the demonstrations and for the violence.

The tone of the meeting began to change when County Sheriff Mel Bailey spoke. He described how the Birmingham jails were filled to capacity and that more arrests would mean using the Legion Field. With his words, Bailey created an ugly portrait of the treasured arena surrounded by a barbed wire fence. This concentration-camp image of Legion Field, Birmingham's famous football stadium, did not sit well with the group.

> With his words, County Sheriff Mel Bailey created an ugly portrait of the treasured stadium surrounded by a barbed wire fence.

And as the businessmen heard police sirens out the window brought on by the downtown demonstrations, they envisioned Birmingham under a martial law imposed by George Wallace. This impression did not seem like the view of Birmingham they wanted the world to see. The committee started to realize they needed to settle with the Southern Christian Leadership Conference (SCLC). They moved closer to acceptable terms and set up a subcommittee to negotiate that evening with members of the African-American community. Right after the discussions, Marshall called President Kennedy. Catching Kennedy at dinner with his brother, Marshall told him, "The meeting worked . . . Now if [it] holds . . . we're over the hump."[3] This was good news to the president, who had earlier told the nation through his assistant press secretary that he was watching the events closely and "continues to hope the situation can be resolved by the people of Birmingham themselves."[4] With Marshall's help, the president's "hope" was being realized.

Negotiations Make Progress and Shuttlesworth Gets Enraged

Black and white teams talked throughout that Tuesday evening and into the morning hours. Early Wednesday, May 8, Lucius Pitts brought the fruits of the negotiating sessions to the Gaston Motel. Essentially, Pitts asked the Gaston group to accept the somewhat vague promise of future changes and the certainty of future negotiations in exchange for halting the demonstrations. After much discussion and some dissent, the group agreed.

And though over one thousand people had gathered in front of the Sixteenth Street Baptist Church and in Kelly Ingram Park, demonstrations were called off for Wednesday. Temperatures rose to 88 degrees. As Young told the press, "It's too hot. We couldn't have controlled this crowd."[5]

In the meantime, Shuttlesworth lay in the hospital, heavily sedated. He wondered why no movement leaders had come to visit, and he worried about what was happening outside. When his doctor realized how stressed the reverend was by being removed from the action, he suggested that

Shuttlesworth return to his room in the Gaston Motel. The reverend agreed, went to the motel, and got into bed. He did not stay in bed long.

Andrew Young arrived and asked that Shuttlesworth come to a meeting with King and others at John Drew's house. Shuttlesworth arrived, still wearing his hospital tags, and wondering aloud why he was called from his sickbed. King hesitantly told him that the African-American negotiating group had decided to call off demonstrations.

The Reverend Fred Shuttlesworth was upset when he heard that the demonstrations had been called off.

Shuttlesworth could not believe what he heard. He sputtered, "Say that again. . . . Did I hear you right? . . . Well Martin, *who* decided? . . . You're in a hell of a fix, young man."[6]

Shuttlesworth let King know that the group could call off the march, but that he would lead the children into the streets once again. As the reverend described this encounter years later, "'Now, that's it. That's it.' I said, 'And if you call it off or Mr. Kennedy calls it off, with the last little ounce of strength I got, I'm gonna get back out and lead.' We had the kids . . . 'bout three thousand of 'em in church. 'I'm gon' lead the last demonstration with what last little ounce I have.'"[7]

Shuttlesworth worried that the negotiators had accepted too little from the white businessmen. With so many people in jail and more ready to march, he felt that more could be gained. As the reverend put it, "Ain't no use scalding the hog on one side! While the water is hot, scald him on both sides and get him clean. If the water gets cold, you ain't *never* gonna clean off that hog."[8] Shuttlesworth stormed out of the Drew house.

Then matters went from bad to worse. Only three hours after King announced that demonstrations would stop in order to permit negotiations to continue, King and Abernathy were rearrested for the charges stemming from their Good Friday protest. Shuttlesworth, sensing an act of bad faith, again grew incensed and was again ready to resume marches. Ultimately, calm and reason prevailed. Robert Kennedy spoke directly with Shuttlesworth and the reverend cooled down. A. G. Gaston posted bail money and got the two ministers out of jail. King and Shuttlesworth talked and agreed to a joint press conference where they announced that the moratorium on demonstrations would continue but that marches would resume the next day if talks failed. And discussions continued that night and resumed on Thursday.

Two Adversaries

The African-American community acted and, as a result, they got through to the president of the United States. President Kennedy started to realize that he had a moral obligation to make civil rights a concern for his presidency and a concern for the American people. At a press conference on Wednesday, May 8, President Kennedy highlighted the

President Kennedy's Statement

During a May 8, 1963 press conference, President John F. Kennedy spoke out in favor of equality for all:

> While much remains to be settled before the situation can be termed satisfactory, we can hope that tensions will ease and that this case history which has so far only narrowly avoided widespread violence and fatalities will remind every State, every community, and every citizen how urgent it is that all bars to equal opportunity and treatment be removed as promptly as possible . . .
>
> I attempted to make clear my strong view that there is an important moral issue involved of equality for all of our citizens. And until you give it to them you are going to have difficulties as we have had this week in Birmingham."[9]

events in Birmingham. The president first commended black and white negotiators. He then warned that there would be other threatening situations if the rights of African Americans were ignored as they had been in Birmingham.

Governor George Wallace disagreed and challenged President Kennedy with an angry rebuttal he released the same day. Wallace praised the "restraint" of the white community, denied Kennedy's accusation that they had mistreated members of the black community, and condemned King for the violence.

The distance between comments made by President Kennedy and Governor Wallace show that there was a major

Wallace's Statement

Governor George Wallace's response to President John F. Kennedy's statement read in part:

> . . . I reject President Kennedy's statement . . . The white people of Birmingham should have been commended for their restraint during the present demonstrations. . . . The President's lack of candor in refusing to criticize the mobs who throw bricks and rocks and bottles and injure authorities and whose clear intent is to incite violence indicates that the President wants us to surrender the state to Martin Luther King . . . The matter of law enforcement must be and shall be left in the hands of constituted authority of the city of Birmingham and this state of Alabama and upon this we shall insist and demand.[10]

rift between Americans over the question of civil rights in 1963 and that much conflict lay ahead.

Final Negotiations

Negotiations continued through Thursday, May 9, and achieved enough success for King to inform reporters at an afternoon press conference, which had been postponed three times throughout the day, that headway made in talks allowed the moratorium on demonstrations to continue. Abernathy warned that if progress did not continue they would all return on Friday "with their marching shoes on."[11] Late Thursday night negotiators reached a final agreement and wording for

Civil rights leaders Martin Luther King, Jr. (left), Fred Shuttlesworth (center), and Ralph Abernathy hold a news conference on May 8, 1963, to suspend demonstrations in Birmingham.

that agreement. One stumbling block remained. Who from the white community would make the announcement the next day? Given the history of violence against those who called for racial equality, the names of the Senior Citizens Committee remained a secret. The white negotiators had genuine fears.

The most conservative and racist elements in the white Birmingham community spoke up. Defeated Mayor Art Hanes told reporters, "if they would stand firm, we would run King and that bunch of race agitators out of town." Concerning the white Senior Citizens Committee he stated, ". . . why are they ashamed to release the names of those on the negotiating committee? Is it because they're ashamed of the fact that they are selling the white folks down the river?" Hanes continued, "They call themselves negotiators. I call them a bunch of quisling, gutless traitors."[12] And no one knew for certain how the twelve hundred police who were now in Birmingham would react to events.

"The Climax of a Long Struggle"

The press conference was called for noon on Friday, May 10, but did not begin until 2:30 P.M. The reporters had been waiting hours. Finally, sitting behind a patio table at the Gaston Motel between King and Abernathy, Shuttlesworth spoke: "The city of Birmingham has reached an accord with its conscience. . . . Birmingham may well offer for Twentieth Century America an example of progressive racial relations; and for all mankind a dawn of a new day, a promise for all men, a day of opportunity, and a new sense of freedom for all America. Thusly, Birmingham may again become a Magic City."[13] Then he laid out the agreement. It included:

> The desegregation of lunchcounters, rest rooms, fitting rooms and drinking fountains in planned stages within the next 90 days. [Fitting rooms would be desegregated on Monday. Thirty days after the new government took

King (left) and Abernathy attend another news conference on May 9, 1963.

office, bathroom and drinking fountain signs would be taken down and sixty days after the new government started its reign, lunch counters would be desegregated.]

The upgrading and hiring of Negroes on a nondiscriminatory basis throughout the industrial community of Birmingham. This will include the hiring of Negroes as clerks and salesmen within the next 60 days . . . [The agreement called for "at least one sales person or cashier" but did not specify if that meant for each store or overall.]

. . . The release of all persons on bond or their personal recognizance. [President Kennedy had helped behind the scenes to obtain bail so that all could be released.]

. . . communications between Negro and white will be publicly reestablished within the next two weeks. We would hope that this channel of communication between the white and Negro communities will prevent the necessity of further protest action or demonstrations.[14] [This biracial committee, set up to discuss employment opportunities and other issues such as the desegregation of parks and schools, would start in fifteen days.]

The New York Times acknowledged, "The settlement terms fell far short of those sought originally by Dr. King and other Negro leaders. They had demanded immediate steps toward desegregation rather than promises."[15]

After the Reverend Shuttlesworth announced the agreement terms, King spoke:

I am very happy to be able to announce that we have come today to the climax of a long struggle for justice, freedom, and human dignity in the City of Birmingham. I say the climax and not the end, for though we have come a long way, there is still a strenuous task before us and some of it is yet uncharted. . . . We seek ultimately a Magic City where color will no longer be the measure of a man's worth, where character will matter more than pigmentation.[16]

King remembered the marching children of Birmingham and their parents when he said, "And without a doubt, the world will never forget the thousands of children and adults who gave up their own physical safety and freedom and went to jail to secure the safety and freedom of all men."[17]

In the middle of the press conference, Shuttlesworth got up and said, "Gentlemen, I hope you will excuse me. I have to go back to the hospital."[18] He then collapsed. His doctor at the segregated hospital where he was taken said that Shuttlesworth was experiencing severe exhaustion, both physical and mental.

It fell to Sidney Smyer to explain the final agreement to the white community. He hoped to convince everyone that the agreement served to avert further violence and was not too radical. Smyer urged calm. As Smyer stated to the public, "It is important that the public understand the steps we have taken were necessary to avoid a dangerous and imminent explosion. . . . We call upon all citizens, white and colored, to

"We call upon all citizens, white and colored, to continue their calm attitude, to stop rumors and to thank God for a chance to reestablish racial peace."

—Sidney Smyer, a white Birmingham business leader involved in settlement negotiations continue their calm attitude, to stop rumors and to thank God for a chance to reestablish racial peace."[19] He said the committee promised nothing to the black community that was "inconsistent with plans which already were in the making before these disturbances."[20] After the announcement, Smyer received a phone call from President Kennedy congratulating him.

Of course, Smyer did not receive praise or support from all corners. Referring to the merchants who had just participated in the negotiations, Bull Connor argued: "The white people and other people of this city should not go in these stores. That's the best way I know to beat down integration in Birmingham."[21] There were other ominous notes. A May 11 *New York Times* article ended its discussion of the day's events with this sentence: "A massive rally of Ku Klux Klansmen from both Alabama and Georgia has been scheduled for tomorrow night just outside the city limits near suburban Bessemer."[22] At the same time, Governor Wallace recalled the state police who had been sent to keep the peace. After speaking at a mass rally on Friday, May 10, Dr. King left the next morning for Atlanta, promising to return on Monday, May 13. At the time, he did not know how much he would be needed.

I call upon all the citizens of Birmingham, both Negro and white, to live up to the standards their responsible leaders set in reaching the agreement of last week to realize that violence only breeds more violence and that good will and good faith are most important now to restore the atmosphere in which last week's agreement can be carried out.[1]

—President John F. Kennedy from a televised speech delivered on May 13, 1963

VIOLENCE
AND MORE
VIOLENCE

Crosses burned as the Ku Klux Klan held a rally to condemn the Birmingham agreement. Over twenty-five hundred people from Alabama and Georgia flocked to the gathering held on Saturday, May 11, 1963, just fifteen miles south of Birmingham. A flier distributed throughout the region drew the crowd: ". . . Knights of the Ku Klux Klan . . . presents a public speaking, 'White Citizens, Know your Rights.' . . . The city of Birmingham and the entire United States of America . . . is under attack. . . . Mongrelizers, beware! The Klan is riding again."[2]

The day started as a family barbecue but soon became much more. The ninety-degree heat did not keep the robed

Klansmen from lighting two twenty-foot-high crosses. Amidst American and Confederate flags, flames rose as people in the crowd chanted "Fight the niggers."[3] Police in their uniforms stood around, not making any arrests.

As evening fell, the throng gathered at a flatbed truck holding the Klan leaders. Imperial Wizard Bobby Shelton spoke. "Good evening, ladies and gentlemen, and fellow Klanspeople." Shelton continued, calling on the crowd to keep from "bowing down to any concessions or demands from any of the atheist so-called ministers of the nigger race or any other group here in Birmingham[4]. . . Martin Luther King has not gained *one thing* in Birmingham, because the white people are not going to tolerate the meddlesome, conniving, manipulating moves of these *professional businessmen*."[5] The families in attendance heard more speeches that night.

> **"Martin Luther King has not gained one thing in Birmingham."**
>
> —Bobby Shelton, a leader of the Ku Klux Klan, a racist organization

As the Klan met, the Gaston Motel received two death threats on the life of Martin Luther King, Jr. There was another warning. Chief Laurie Prichett, the Albany, Georgia, sheriff who had come to Birmingham to see if King planned to return to Albany, urged local police to take special care when Klan rallies followed civil rights settlements. He encouraged them to protect King carefully. Connor retorted he would not protect King at all.[6]

The First Bombing of the Night

Tired after attending one more church rally on the night of May 11, the Reverend A. D. King, Martin Luther King, Jr.'s brother, came home and went to bed. His wife, Naomi, sat in the living room as the Kings' five children slept in their rooms. A car sped by their ranch house. The first bomb detonated in the King home at 10:45 P.M., thirty minutes after the Klan rally ended. The family quickly gathered and were heading out the back door when the second bomb exploded. Given the amount of destruction, it is amazing that no one was hurt. As one observer later described:

> Glass and broken timbers were strewn about on the floor. Nearly every window in the building was broken. What remained of the front end was lit only by police flashlights. There was a large crater, five feet across and three feet deep where the front porch once had been. . . . The living room is completely, absolutely demolished.[7]

The explosion blew off the brick veneer from the front of the house and shoved the front door through the living room. A.D. phoned his brother Martin to convey the news, both bad and good. "They just bombed the house. But thank God, we are all safe."[8]

An angry crowd of a thousand soon gathered. So did police and firemen. *The New York Times* reported, "While the authorities inspected the ruins, spectators slashed and punctured the tires on police and fire vehicles with knives and icepicks."[9] Someone threw burning paper into the front seat of a patrol car. Others hurled rocks. Some just yelled insults at the police. King emerged from the damage of his

The Reverend A. D. King (second from left) surveys the damage done to his home by a dynamite blast. Another civil rights leader, Wyatt Tee Walker, is second from the right.

house and begged the mob to be nonviolent. Church deacons moved through the scene, encouraging the people to sing freedom songs.

The Second Bombing of the Night

Close to midnight, the people at the A. D. King home heard another blast. King exclaimed, "Oh, my God. That's my church." Wyatt Tee Walker, helping the reverend to calm the crowd, corrected him: "That's the motel."[10]

At 11:58 P.M. a car containing four men with darkened faces drove past the Gaston Motel. A bomb thrown from the car landed between the motel and a lot with trailers. The bombers missed their intended target, Suite 30, where Martin Luther King, Jr., had been staying.

The noise scared workers and patrons who were inside the building. "Diners and waitresses began screaming. Some started to run into the street."[11] Isaac Reynolds, an activist staying in the motel, was in bed watching television the night of the bombing when:

> About ten minutes to twelve, I heard a tremendous explosion and my glasses on my dresser were knocked off and I was thrown out of my bed. It threw my door open, which was locked at the time. I got up and came out and found the lobby of the motel cloudy with smoke.[12]

The explosion "blew a hole in a downstairs motel room, damaged the motel office and shattered windows in the motel and J. D.'s Grocery nearby." Reynolds went down to the blasted room and found the manager's sister in the room, now with a hole in the wall and the door blown off. Luckily, she survived

Above is wreckage from a bomb explosion at the Gaston Motel where Dr. Martin Luther King, Jr., and other leaders of the Southern Christian Leadership Conference (SCLC) were staying in Birmingham.

the blast. Throughout the motel, only four people were slightly injured. Beyond the damage to the motel office, the three trailers in the next door lot were "buckled and twisted."[13]

The police had plenty of warning. Ben Allen, a Birmingham policeman, explained, "I had information that the Gaston Motel in Birmingham was gonna be dynamited at a given hour from an informer that had never given me wrong information before. . . ."[14] Allen promptly told Colonel Lingo, commander of the Alabama Highway Patrol. Lingo ignored the message. And it seemed strange that the state troopers who had been patrolling the streets just hours before the motel was hit were nowhere in sight when the bomb went off. They returned right after the explosion.

A Night of Rioting

At the sound of the bomb, local bars, nightclubs, and pool halls emptied. Patrons poured into the streets surrounding the motel. Nearby Kelly Ingram Park soon filled with two thousand people. This Saturday-night crowd did not hold the same nonviolent philosophy preached by the reverends King and Shuttlesworth. They met every police car that came into the area with projectiles, including coke bottles and bricks, and with screams of "Kill 'em! Kill 'em!"[15] A white-owned taxicab was turned over and a local Italian-owned grocery store was set on fire.

Eventually, the firemen showed up, but the mob did not permit them to get to the buildings. The fire spread to adjacent houses and then to a two-story apartment building. One whole block of buildings caught on fire. Cars parked in front of the Sixteenth Street Baptist Church were overturned and burned. Rioting was already so intense that five policemen had been sent to the hospital, including one with a serious knife wound.

Wyatt Tee Walker and the Reverend A. D. King also sped to the scene at the Gaston Motel. Walker, wearing a white

The Reverend Wyatt Tee Walker, integration leader of the SCLC, stands atop a car while speaking with a megaphone to calm a crowd gathered shortly after midnight on May 12, 1963, after bombing attacks on the Gaston Motel and A. D. King's home.

handkerchief on his sleeve to signify peace, got on top of a car with a bullhorn and begged everyone to go home. He told them, "Please do not throw any bricks any more."[16] In the park, King told the crowd, "Our *home* was just bombed. . . . Now . . . if we have gone away *not* angry, *not* throwing bricks, . . . why must you rise up to hurt our cause. You are hurting us. . . . Now won't you *please* clear the park."[17] The crowd did not seem to listen. Some chanted, "Eye for an eye, tooth for a tooth."[18] Others wondered aloud, "How come *we* have to go home every time *they* start violence?"[19] Despite the mob's rage, King, Walker, and other SCLC leaders managed to quiet the people down with their appeals. The calm did not last long.

Colonel Al Lingo with two hundred fifty Alabama state police and the posse of deputized and armed volunteers brought in by Sheriff Jim Clark stormed through the crowd. The people's anger mushroomed. Jamie Moore, chief of police in Birmingham, relieved that the rioting had died down, looked at Lingo's automatic shotgun and stated, "If you'd leave, Mr. Lingo, I'd appreciate it."

The state director of public safety responded, "I'm not going to leave. I've been sent here by the governor and I'm going to stay."

Mr. Moore said again, "If you'd leave, Mr. Lingo I'd appreciate it."

Moore continued, "Those guns are not needed. Will you please put them up? Somebody's going to get killed."

"You're damned right it'll get somebody killed," Lingo told him.[20]

Colonel Al Lingo

Colonel Al Lingo served as Alabama director of public safety from 1963–1965, under Governor George Wallace. He had close ties to the governor, sharing the governor's views on race. As Lingo told a *New York Times* reporter: "I am not a Nigra-Hater. I've played with 'em, I've eaten with 'em and I've worked with 'em, but I still believe in segregation."[21] Colonel Lingo was known for his vicious assaults on civil rights demonstrators.

It was 2:30 A.M. when the reinforcements walked down the streets with their shotguns and carbines. Jim Clark and his troops rode in on horseback. They charged into the courtyard at the motel and as *The New York Times* reported, "The 'thonk' of clubs striking heads could be heard across the street."[22] Lingo and the troopers went down the street assaulting African Americans. This is how *Newsweek* conveyed the scene:

> **Up and down the street they went, shoving and clubbing spectators, clomping up on front porches, swatting bystanders with billies and gun butts, ordering: "Get inside, goddamit!" "I can't, I can't, the door's locked," one Negro screamed as police walloped him. The troopers dashed the door open with gun butts and shoved him inside.**[23]

Besides Lingo's troops, Bull Connor's tank roamed the streets. The assault from the various law enforcement agencies refueled African-American rage and rioting renewed. It was five o'clock in the morning before peace finally prevailed.

On the morning of Sunday, May 12, Colonel Lingo sealed off a twenty-eight-block area, letting in only residents and officials. Police stopped and searched drivers attempting to get into the sector. Much of the damage wrought the previous night could now be clearly seen. One *New York Times* headline read: "9-Block Area Lies Devastated; Buildings Still Burn After Riot." In the previous night, beyond the destruction done to the Gaston Motel and King's home, seven small stores and two apartment buildings had burned to the ground. Dozen of cars, including police cars, had been destroyed and fifty people had been injured during the night's activities.

President Kennedy Gets Involved

From Washington, President Kennedy feared that the riots would lead to an unraveling of the agreement. To find out how firm the settlement was, Burke Marshall made important inquiries for the president. First, he called Sid Smyer. Smyer told him that the Senior Citizens Committee would lay low for a few days, but they would stick to the deal. In light of the two bombings, Kennedy was even more concerned about how King and SCLC would respond. Would they view the bombings as just one more betrayal and go back to marching in the streets? President Kennedy asked Marshall about King's intentions. Marshall told the president:

> I'll tell you what he intends to do, Mr. President. He intends to go to this church and call upon his people to [stay off the streets] . . . And then tomorrow, he intends to go around the city and visit pool halls and saloons and talk to the Negroes, and preach against violence. Those are his intentions.[24]

Assistant Attorney General Burke Marshall found out what the mood in Birmingham was like and reported back to President Kennedy. He found that the possibility of more violence was high.

With the pact safe for the moment, the administration needed to make sure the bloodshed in Birmingham would not continue. Violence could come from several sources including the Klan, an angered African-American community, or, of most concern for Kennedy, Governor Wallace, and Colonel Lingo's troopers. All of these concerns weighed on President Kennedy's mind.

Kennedy met with key advisers on Sunday, May 12, and mapped out a plan. First, to make sure talking would continue, if needed, Burke Marshall went back to Birmingham. Next, Kennedy and his advisers set up a military response. Federal troops "trained in riot control" were sent to army bases near the city of Birmingham. Kennedy also nationalized the Alabama Guard and got them ready to go in if peace failed. Finally, and perhaps most importantly, President Kennedy started to think seriously about federal legislation that would end segregation and promote civil rights throughout the United States.

President Kennedy knew that he needed to explain his move to the people of the South and the rest of the nation.

On the night of Monday, May 13, he went on television and said the following:

> This Government will do whatever must be done to preserve order, to protect the lives of its citizens and to uphold the law of the land. . . . The Birmingham agreement was and is a fair and just accord. . . . I call upon all citizens of Birmingham, both Negro and white, to live up to the standards their responsible leaders set in reaching the agreement of last week to realize that violence only breeds more violence and that good will and good faith are most important now to restore the atmosphere in which last week's agreement can be carried out.[25]

Then the President laid out the three steps he was taking to help keep the peace. These steps included sending Burke Marshall back to Birmingham, stationing federal troops in bases around the city, and nationalizing the state guard.

Two calm heads prevailed in support of the president's efforts at protecting the agreement. First, King had returned immediately to Birmingham and told the people at a Sunday, May 12, evening rally, "We must work passionately and unrelentingly for first-class citizenship, but we must not use second-class methods to gain it."[26] To clarify his faith in the settlement, he told reporters, "I do not feel the events of last night nullified the agreement at all."[27] And Sidney Smyer agreed. On Monday, May 13, he held a press conference to reinforce his commitment and the Mules' commitment to the accord. So far, concord between the two sides remained.

Governor Wallace Responds

Governor Wallace, on the other hand, seemed intent on disrupting the peace process. First of all, he sent a telegram to President Kennedy, in which he questioned constitutional authority for sending troops and expressed further resentment at the action:

> **In my judgment your duty is to guarantee the right of this State and the City of Birmingham to handle their own domestic affairs, and any intervention into the affairs of this State or the City of Birmingham, whether by the use of National Military troops or otherwise, is in direct violation of your constitutional obligation.**[28]

In a statement on Sunday, May 12, Governor Wallace stirred the pot even further by suggesting that the leaders in the civil rights movement, who he often accused of being Communist, were responsible for the previous night's violence: "Violence and internal disorder are the stock and trade of the Communists, and in my judgment there has been sufficient activity in Alabama by outside subversives to strongly indicate their involvement in the bombing incident." He further expressed his disdain for those who worked on the settlement: "The so-called biracial negotiating group of appeasers who have kept their identity secret, have played right into the hands of Martin Luther King, Jr., and his cohorts, who had failed to bring strife and turmoil to the extent they desired."[29]

King Visits the Poolhalls of Birmingham

King wanted to make sure that if turbulence came, it would not come from the black community. On Monday, May 13, he toured the bars and poolrooms of Birmingham urging nonviolence. As one observer described, "At the smoke-filled New Home Billiard Parlor, the staccato clickety-clack of the cue sticks and pool balls was mingling with the mournful moan of a rock 'n roll record when King arrived. . . . The talk was boisterous, the language far from the kind you hear in church."[30] King started his visit to one poolhall by losing a game of pool. Referring to the angry violence from many in the black community on Saturday night, he then spoke to the gathered crowd as if he were at a church rally:

> **Now I can understand how impatient we are. . . . how we are often driven to the brink of bitterness and even despair, because of the way we are treated by policemen. . . . and the way we are bombed . . . but we must make it clear that it is possible to stand up against all of these evils and injustices without fighting back with violence. . . . We must not beat up any policemen . . . We have the power of our souls, the power of our standing up together and this amazing unity and this soul force are the things that will free us in this day.[31]**

The visit ended with the gathering of weapons and then with King, his SCLC colleagues, and the poolhall crowd linking their arms and singing, "We shall overcome!" As King went from site to site, well wishers accompanied him on his pilgrimage. State troopers carrying carbines followed the group. King had gone to two pool halls and, with the crowd swelling to one hundred, was on his way to a third when the troopers ordered all to "reverse and go back the way you came."[32] King returned to the Gaston Motel where he was staying. One young man who observed the troopers and saw

Breaking the Color Barrier

Jackie Robinson was the first African American to play Major League Baseball. Though an excellent player, he is best known for the character he displayed in not responding to the slurs of fans and fellow players. Out of respect for his significant achievement, his number, 42, was retired from baseball. After leaving baseball, Robinson continued to push for African-American civil rights.

them shove some bystanders out of the way told a reporter, "I don't care what King says. I don't give a damn about that nonviolence stuff."[33]

That evening the community rallied at Sixth Avenue Baptist Church. Two thousand attended. Floyd Patterson, the boxer, and Jackie Robinson spoke. This is what Jackie Robinson said: "I don't think you realize down here in Birmingham what you mean to us up there in New York. And I don't think white Americans understand what Birmingham means to all of us throughout the country."[34] He told the crowd that his own children wanted to come to Alabama so that they too could go to jail. Then Dr. King spoke, proclaiming, "I am convinced that the agreements that have been made will be met. . . . We *must* have faith in our movement."[35]

Over the course of the next week, the city remained calm. The federal troops surrounding Birmingham stayed in their bases. For the moment, there were no more bombs and no more riots.

The Courts Rule

On Monday, May 20, the Birmingham Board of Education expelled one thousand kids who had participated in the demonstrations. This meant that the expelled students would need to go to summer school in order to graduate. The National Association for the Advancement of Colored People (NAACP) filed a suit in support of the students and lost. James Bevel began organizing a boycott of the schools and a boycott of local businesses. King again returned to Birmingham and spoke against the boycott, fearing it would threaten the settlement. Luckily, the NAACP appealed to a higher court and won, halting the expulsions.

The day after the ruling in support of the kids, there was more good news. The Alabama Supreme Court handed down their ruling on Birmingham's election and declared Albert Boutwell the winner. The reign of Theophilus Eugene "Bull" Connor had ended.

> **"I don't think white Americans understand what Birmingham means to all of us throughout the country."**
>
> —Jackie Robinson, first African American to play Major League Baseball

We'll march to freedom tomorrow. To our parents, we say, "We wish you'd come along with us. But, if you won't, at least don't try to stop us."[1]

—Cleveland Donald, a high school junior speaking to a mass rally the day six hundred young people were arrested in Jackson, Mississippi

"DON'T TRY TO STOP US"

When the children of Birmingham marched, they inspired many others. Young people elsewhere joined the fight. Take Jackson, Mississippi for example. Throughout May 1963, youth in the city headed for the streets. They protested against segregation and discrimination in a manner that mirrored their Birmingham peers. As one reporter described:

> The students, singing freedom songs, and waving American flags and picket signs, had marched through the city toward the downtown shopping area. City policemen, state highway patrolmen and sheriff's deputies, many of them carrying riot guns, formed a double line and headed off the students. The children refused to disperse. They waited in orderly lines to be arrested.[2]

During that protest, the police arrested six hundred kids, took them away in trucks, and jailed them at the state fairgrounds. The night of the march, Cleveland Donald, a high school junior, told people at a mass rally, "We'll march to freedom tomorrow. To our parents, we say, 'We wish you'd come along with us. But, if you won't, at least don't try to stop us.'"[3] Like their counterparts in Birmingham, the young people of Jackson continued to demonstrate and they continued to fill up the jails.

At North Carolina Agricultural and Technical State University in Greensboro, twenty-one-year-old student-body president Jesse Jackson made explicit the inspiration of the Birmingham movement saying, "When a police dog bites us in Birmingham, people of color bleed all over America."[4] From April through June, the students from the college marched against segregated facilities (theaters and restaurants) and got arrested in droves. After one May demonstration with 400 arrests, students were crammed into a shutdown polio hospital ward meant for 125. Demonstrations in Greensboro seemed to capture the spirit of Birmingham as this Associated Press description of a June protest suggests: "Mass arrests were resumed here tonight as hundreds of singing, hand-clapping Negroes paraded through the downtown section and sat down in the middle of the main intersection."[5] Police arrested 278 who were sitting in the street.[6]

And then there was Savannah, Georgia. In June, "400 singing, clapping youthful Negroes staged a 'Freedom march'"[7] to downtown Savannah and demanded an end to the segregation of public facilities. Fifty staged sit-ins at segregated restaurants and hotels and got arrested. On the next day, demonstrations almost grew into a riot when police used tear gas before hauling off 261 demonstrators including 200 juveniles.[8] Because jails were already so full, officials placed the demonstrators in stockades near the airport.

The numbers for those going to jail mounted. One hundred teens from Americus, Georgia, sitting in at a local theater got arrested. Subsequent demonstrations in Americus grew into violent confrontations with officials. Police in Tallahassee, Florida, teargassed and arrested 257 young marchers from local high schools and colleges who were also protesting against segregated facilities.[9] In Gadsden, Alabama, a student march memorializing slain civil rights activist William Moore led to the jailing of seven hundred.[10] Overall, after the marches in Birmingham the country experienced a staggering level of civil rights activity. Throughout May and early June alone there were 758 protests in 186 cities which led to the arrest of 14,733 people.[11] Clearly, the spirit unleashed by the children of Birmingham moved many people.

President Kennedy and Civil Rights

As protests captured the nation's attention, civil rights became an issue that President Kennedy and members of his administration could no longer ignore. Because of Birmingham and pressure brought by subsequent and seemingly nonstop demonstrations, Burke Marshall and other presidential advisers came to a conclusion, "We've got to have the [civil rights] bill."[12] Marshall saw no other way to stop the relentless marching, which he feared would lead to disorder and violence rather than the passage of important laws. He therefore urged President Kennedy to champion a civil rights bill that directly addressed the issue of segregation in the South and more. The president agreed. And though the fear of violence was prominent in the president's thoughts, he also viewed the need for a civil rights law in moral terms. After much discussion behind closed doors, the drive to pass the new bill began with an important televised address on June 11, 1963. In the speech, President Kennedy paid homage to the Birmingham movement when he said, "The events in Birmingham and elsewhere have so increased the cries for equality that no city or state or legislative body can prudently choose to ignore them." He went on:

> The fires of frustration and discord are burning in every city, North and South, where legal remedies are not at hand. Redress is sought in the streets, in demonstrations, parades, and protests which create tensions and threaten violence and threaten lives.
>
> We face, therefore, a moral crisis as a country and a people. It cannot be met by repressive police action. It cannot be left to increased demonstrations in the streets. . . .
>
> I am, therefore, asking the Congress to enact legislation giving all Americans the right to be served in facilities which are open to the public—hotels, restaurants, theaters, retail stores, and similar establishments.[13]

On June 20, 1963, Representative Emmanuel Celler from New York introduced a bill in the House of Representatives that would eventually become the Civil Rights Act of 1964. By submitting the law, Celler made many goals of the Birmingham movement into national goals.

Back to Birmingham

Ironically, as the rest of the country started to move forward, progress slowed down in Birmingham. Early signs of problems came on May 13, when Sidney Smyer claimed that the agreement required stores to promote only one black worker overall as opposed to one for each store. Leaders such as Shuttlesworth saw this as a betrayal and screamed foul.

In July things went downhill further. Mayor Boutwell set up the agreed upon biracial committee to continue discussions about civil rights in Birmingham and named it the Citizens Affairs Committee (CAC). Unfortunately, the CAC's committee structure was set up in a manner that limited the power of African Americans. Despite concerns from the black community, David Vann saw a silver lining. Observing white supremacists picketing the first meeting, Vann noted, "These leaders of Birmingham walked through the lines of the Ku Klux Klan demonstrators and held their meeting; they refused to be intimidated and I believe that was one of those very critical times again as we went forward in that summer."[14]

Another hopeful sign came on July 23. Birmingham repealed all of their segregation laws, outlawing segregation in public accommodations including restaurants, hotels, and motels. Activists soon successfully tested the repeal of those laws in many establishments. And the push for civil rights intensified throughout the nation.

A March on Washington

As the civil rights bill headed to Congress, King and other civil rights leaders began to discuss the follow-up to Birmingham.

They concluded that the best action would be a massive march in Washington, D.C. Through the march, they hoped to demand equal economic opportunity for African Americans, to support and push for President Kennedy's civil rights bill, and to keep civil rights on everyone's mind. The leaders set August 28 as the day for the March on Washington, just three-and-a-half months after the Birmingham marches had ended.

On August 27 and August 28, people poured in on buses and trains from all over the country. As a *New York Times* headline aptly put it, "Capital is Occupied by Gentle Army." The day's events received continuous live television coverage by CBS and lesser coverage by ABC and NBC. Television made the civil rights movement available to the home of every American and all could be witness to the 250,000 who filled the space from the Lincoln Memorial to the Washington Monument.[15]

Just before noon, eager marchers spontaneously started the procession toward the Lincoln Memorial. Speeches given by civil rights leaders, labor leaders, and religious leaders then followed the march. The final oration—"I have a dream"—was delivered by Martin Luther King, Jr. Through television, King's words entered the homes of many Americans, including the homes of many white Americans. Though he had written the speech the night before, moved by the day's events and by reactions from the audience, King improvised final portions of his talk, including his "I have a dream" remarks.

The marchers left Washington as quickly as they had come into the city. *The New York Times* reported, "At 9 P.M. the city was as calm as the waters of the Reflecting Pool between the

Immortal Words

The most powerful part of Dr. Martin Luther King's "I Have a Dream" speech reads as follows:

I have a dream that one day this nation will rise up and live out the true meaning of its creed: "We hold these truths to be self-evident, that all men are created equal."

I have a dream that one day on the red hills of Georgia, the sons of former slaves and the sons of former slave owners will be able to sit down together at the table of brotherhood. . . .

I have a dream that my four little children will one day live in a nation where they will not be judged by the color of their skin but by the content of their character. I have a dream today!

I have a dream that one day down in Alabama, with its vicious racists, with its governor having his lips dripping with the words of "interposition" and "nullification," one day right there in Alabama little black boys and black girls will be able to join hands with little white boys and white girls as sisters and brothers. I have a dream today.

And so let freedom ring from the prodigious hilltops of New Hampshire. Let freedom ring from the mighty mountains of New York. . . . But not only that. Let freedom ring from Stone Mountain of Georgia. . . .

And when this happens, when we allow freedom to ring, when we let it ring from every village and every hamlet, from every state and every city, we will be able to speed up that day when all of God's children, black men and white men, Jews and Gentiles, Protestants and Catholics, will be able to join hands and sing in the words of the old Negro spiritual:

"Free at last! Free at last!
Thank God Almighty, we are free at last!"[16]

The Reverend Martin Luther King, Jr., waves to the crowd in Washington, D.C., on August 28, 1963, the day he gave his "I Have a Dream" speech.

two memorials."[17] The day ended with a meeting at the White House between Kennedy and march leaders.

More Bombings in Birmingham

With spirits high and the movement in full force, the pendulum swung back to a sense of despair as the nation's eyes turned once again to Birmingham. In early September, five black children integrated three all-white elementary schools in Birmingham. Elements in the white community were very unhappy about this push for integration and expressed their anger by twice bombing the home of Arthur Shores, a black Birmingham attorney active in the civil rights movement. Then things got much worse.

It was September 15 and four young girls—Addie Mae Collins, fourteen; Denise McNair, eleven; Carole Robertson, fourteen; and Cynthia Wesley, fourteen—were in the basement restroom of the Sixteenth Street Baptist Church excitedly discussing the start of the school year. The girls, all dressed in white, had just come from their Sunday school class where they had heard a lesson on the topic "The love that forgives." They were getting ready to lead church services. Sarah Collins, Addie's sister, was in the restroom with the four others and recalls, "I remember Denise asking Addie to tie her belt. Addie was tying her sash. Then it happened."[18] At 10:22, a bomb detonated at the church, killing Addie, Denise, Carole, and Cynthia, injuring twenty others, and shocking the world. Sarah went on, "I couldn't see anymore because my eyes were full of glass—twenty-three pieces of glass. I didn't know

The bombing of the Sixteenth Street Baptist Church in Birmingham on September 15, 1963, left four girls dead.

what happened. I just remember calling 'Addie, Addie.' But there was no answer. I don't remember any pain. I just remember wanting Addie."[19] After spending three months in the hospital, Sarah did survive, losing the sight in her right eye.

The bombing severely damaged the church itself. As reported in *The New York Times*, "The blast blew gaping holes through walls in the church basement. Floors of offices in the rear of the sanctuary appeared near collapse. Stairways were blocked by splintered window frames, glass and timbers."[20]

From the left are Denise McNair, eleven; Carole Robertson, fourteen; Addie Mae Collins, fourteen; and Cynthia Wesley, fourteen.

The Klan had bombed the Church in order to slow down or stop the civil rights movement. The tragedy had the opposite effect. The nation experienced in a very direct, painful manner why legislation was needed to protect the rights of African Americans.

King spoke these words at the funeral for three of the four girls: ". . . life is hard, at times as hard as crucible steel."[21] Feeling that hardness, Diane Nash Bevel, a movement leader, proposed a major action that would effectively shut down the entire state of Alabama. King did not go along with the plan. President Kennedy, fearing violence in Birmingham, sent Burke Marshall back to Alabama to see what needed to be done and issued a statement condemning the bombing. King and leaders from the Birmingham community met with the president. Meanwhile, the push for civil rights legislation intensified.

Two Pieces of Legislation

Americans experienced another shock two months later when President Kennedy was shot dead. After President Kennedy's assassination in November 1963, Vice President Lyndon Johnson became the new president. People wondered if a southern politician would have the same passion for civil rights as his predecessor. Many were therefore surprised when Johnson told the nation, ". . . no memorial oration or eulogy could more eloquently honor President Kennedy's memory than the earliest passage of the civil rights bill for which he fought so long."[22] President Johnson worked hard to see that a strong measure got passed.

On July 2, President Johnson signed the Civil Rights Act of 1964 into law. The bill accomplished three things. First, the act outlawed segregation in public life including restaurants, hotels, movie theaters, and more. Second, it forced the federal government to actively end segregation within public schools. Finally, the bill banned discrimination in hiring that was based on race, color, religion, national origin, or gender. The bill accomplished for the nation what movement leaders had sought to accomplish in Birmingham.

As passage of the Civil Rights Act drew near, the Boutwell government in Birmingham created a document that laid out procedures for complying with the new law. First of all, they worked closely with the white business community, discussing with them what the law would mean. Secondly, they offered the protection of local police for all who voluntarily followed the law. The day after the bill was passed, Shuttlesworth and his followers spread throughout the community to test the impact of the law. To their surprise, they were served at local restaurants, including Brittling's Cafeteria, the scene of sit-ins the previous year. And they were able to sit where they chose at local movie houses. The owner of Ollie's, a local barbecue joint in Birmingham, challenged the law and took his challenge all the way to the Supreme Court. He lost. Compliance with the section of the act calling for integration of public facilities came quickly to Birmingham.

And when it was clear that the new legislation was not strong enough to guarantee the right to vote, Birmingham-style demonstrations continued throughout the South in 1964 and 1965, leading to passage of the Voting Rights Act of 1965. On August 6, 1965, President Johnson signed the Voting Rights Act, ending practices which kept African Americans from voting and setting up procedures that would dramatically increase the number of African-American voters in the country, especially in the South.

The passage of the Voting Rights Act added about fifty-thousand new African-American voters to the voting lists of Birmingham by 1966.[23] In 1971, Birmingham had its first

The Reverend Fred Shuttlesworth gives a sermon at the Greater New Life Baptist Church in Cincinnati, Ohio, on March 19, 2006. He helped start the church three years after his contribution to the Birmingham civil rights movement.

black council member and in 1979, its first black mayor. The laws, which had come about as a direct and indirect result of the Birmingham demonstrations, made certain that the essence of the movement's goals would be reached.

The Birmingham Legacy

Young people in Birmingham and elsewhere were a vital part of the civil rights movement. This should come as no surprise given that Jim Crow and injustice affected all members of the African-American community, including its children. Dr. Martin Luther King, Jr., reminds the nation of this pain in his letter from Birmingham Jail:

> . . . when you suddenly find your tongue twisted . . . as you seek to explain to your six-year-old daughter why she can't go to the public amusement park that has just been advertised on television, and see tears welling up in her eyes when she is told that Funtown is closed to colored children, and see ominous clouds of inferiority beginning to form in her little mental sky, and see her beginning to distort her personality by developing an unconscious bitterness toward white people; when you have to concoct an answer for a five-year-old son, who is asking: "Daddy, why do white people treat colored people so mean?" . . . [24]

From segregated schools to the ubiquitous "colored" and "white" signs marking off the black facilities from the white facilities, African-American children understood that they were included in the cloud of injustice and needed to be a part of the struggle to fight that injustice. They marched with a full heart and they made a difference.

On May 8, 1963, five teenagers speak at a news conference in Birmingham about mistreatment they say they received following arrests during demonstrations.

History often seems to be the record of only what adults have done to shape the world, and that false impression suggests that the younger generation has little to do with the important changes in history. The young people of Birmingham remind us that the next generation is very much a part of this planet and can affect the direction the planet takes. When the children of Birmingham marched in 1963, they helped historians write "a marvelous chapter" and they might even move children forty or fifty years in their future to fight for a better world and to continue the Birmingham story.[25]

1947 — Jackie Robinson integrates Major League Baseball by becoming a Brooklyn Dodger.

1954 — In the case *Brown* v. *Board of Education*, the Supreme Court overturns the earlier decision in *Plessy* v. *Ferguson* and rules that segregation in public schooling violates the Constitution. The justices state directly that "separate educational facilities are inherently unequal."

1955 –1956 — Rosa Parks refuses to give up her bus seat to a white person and ignites a yearlong boycott of buses by the African-American community in Montgomery, Alabama. This fight for integration is led by the young and then unknown minister, Martin Luther King, Jr.

1956 — After the National Association for the Advancement of Colored People (NAACP) is banned in Alabama, the Reverend Fred Shuttlesworth works with others in the Birmingham community to start the Alabama Christian Movement for Human Rights (ACMHR).

The Klan bombs the home of Shuttlesworth in Birmingham. Shuttlesworth ignores the warning and continues to fight for the integration of buses.

1957 — King and other activists found the Southern Christian Leadership Conference (SCLC).

A mob savagely beats Shuttlesworth when he tries to enroll his daughters at all-white Phillips High School.

1960 — Four African-American college students sit-in at a Woolworth's lunch counter in Greensboro, North Carolina, and fuel a movement that inspires other students throughout the South to fight for the integration of facilities.

Growing from the Greensboro sit-ins, young activists form the Student Nonviolent Coordinating Committee (SNCC).

1961 — An integrated group of thirteen freedom riders boards buses in Washington, D.C., and travels throughout the South in order to desegregate transportation facilities. The riders are met and beaten by mobs in Birmingham.

1961 –1962 — SCLC and SNCC lead unsuccessful demonstrations against segregation in Albany, Georgia.

1962 — James Meredith integrates the University of Mississippi. President Kennedy sends in federal troops to quell riots.

1963 — **January:** Shuttlesworth invites SCLC to Birmingham to support the fight against segregation.

April: Dr. Martin Luther King, Jr., arrives in Birmingham. The first demonstrations and marches slowly begin.

April 12: On Good Friday, King and the Reverend Ralph Abernathy violate a court injunction against marching and are arrested.

Late April: In response to white clergy who question the need for demonstrations, King composes his famous "Letter from Birmingham Jail."

Early May: In support of the movement, young people skip school and march in the streets of Birmingham. They fill the jails.

May 10: Representatives of the white community in Birmingham reach a settlement with SCLC.

May 11: One day after the settlement is announced, the Klan bombs the home of Martin Luther King, Jr.'s brother, the Reverend A. D. King, as well as the Gaston Motel. Rioting erupts throughout Birmingham.

June 11: In a major television address, President John F. Kennedy calls for significant civil rights legislation.

August 28: Over two hundred fifty thousand march in Washington to support the goals of the civil rights movement. Marchers hear Martin Luther King, Jr., deliver his famous "I have a dream" speech.

September 15: The Klan bombs the Sixteenth Street Baptist Church killing four young girls and shocking the nation.

November 22: President Kennedy is assassinated in Dallas.

1964 — Congress passes the Civil Rights Act of 1964, which includes many of the same goals sought by SCLC and ACMHR through the Birmingham marches.

1965 — Congress passes the Voting Rights Act of 1965, which leads to a dramatic increase in the number of African-American voters.

1979 — Richard Arrington becomes the first African-American mayor of Birmingham, Alabama.

CHAPTER 1. "Blown Into History"

1. Andrew M. Manis, *A Fire You Can't Put Out: The Civil Rights Life of Birmingham's Fred Shuttlesworth* (Tuscaloosa, Ala.: The University of Alabama Press, 1999), p. 109.
2. Ellen Levine, *Freedom's Children: Young Civil Rights Activists Tell Their Own Stories* (New York: Puffin Books, 2000), p. 7.
3. Ibid., p. 9.
4. Manis, p. 110.
5. Lewis W. Jones, "Fred L. Shuttlesworth, Indigenous Leader" in David J. Garrow, Jr., ed., *Birmingham Alabama, 1956–1963: The Black Struggle for Civil Rights* (Brooklyn, New York: Carson Publishing, Inc., 1989), pp. 137–138.
6. Harrison E. Salisbury, "Fear and Hatred Grip Birmingham," *The New York Times*, April 12, 1960, pp. 1, 28.
7. Martin Luther King, Jr., *Why We Can't Wait* (New York: Signet Books, 2000), p. 36.
8. Howell Raines, *My Soul is Rested: The Story of the Civil Rights Movement in the Deep South* (New York: G. P. Putnam's Sons, 1977), pp. 139–140.
9. Levine, p. 6.
10. Ibid.
11. Ibid., p. 12.
12. Glenn T. Eskew, *But for Birmingham: The Local and National Movements in the Civil Rights Struggle* (Chapel Hill, N.C.: University of North Carolina Press, 1997), p. 53.
13. Manis, p. 114.
14. Ibid.
15. Ibid., p. 109.
16. Diane McWhorter, *Carry Me Home: Birmingham, Alabama: The Climactic Battle of the Civil Rights Revolution* (New York: Touchstone, 2001), p. 115.

CHAPTER 2. The Reverend Shuttlesworth Fights On

1. Andrew M. Manis, *A Fire You Can't Put Out: The Civil Rights Life of Birmingham's Fred Shuttlesworth* (Tuscaloosa, Ala.: The University of Alabama Press, 1999), p. 153.

2. Ibid., p. 156.
3. Ellen Levine, *Freedom's Children: Young Civil Rights Activists Tell Their Own Stories* (New York: Puffin Books, 2000), p. 37.
4. Fred L. Shuttlesworth, "Birmingham Revisited: Minister Returns to City to View Decade of Change," *Ebony*, August 1971, p. 115.
5. Ibid.
6. Manis, p. 153.
7. Glenn T. Eskew, "The Alabama Christian Movement for Human Rights and the Birmingham Struggle for Civil Rights, 1956–1963" in David J. Garrow, Jr., ed., *Birmingham Alabama, 1956–1963: The Black Struggle for Civil Rights* (Brooklyn, New York: Carson Publishing, Inc., 1989), p. 16.
8. Glenn T. Eskew, *But for Birmingham: The Local and National Movements in the Civil Rights Struggle* (Chapel Hill, N.C.: University of North Carolina Press, 1997), pp. 165–166.
9. Ibid., p. 157.
10. Shuttlesworth, p. 116.
11. Eskew, p. 157.
12. Shuttlesworth, p. 117.

CHAPTER 3. The Movement Begins

1. Howell Raines, *My Soul is Rested: The Story of the Civil Rights Movement in the Deep South* (New York: G. P. Putnam's Sons, 1977), p. 156.
2. Henry Hampton and Steve Fayer, *Voices of Freedom: An Oral History of the Civil Rights Movement from the 1950s through the 1980s* (New York: Bantam Books, 1990), p. 125.
3. David J. Garrow, *Bearing the Cross: Martin Luther King, Jr., and the Southern Christian Leadership Conference* (New York: Quill, 1986), p. 229.
4. Raines, p. 144.
5. Jocelyn Ulrich, "'We Were the Heart of the Struggle:' Women in the Birmingham Civil Rights Movement," *Senior Thesis, Russell Sage College*, <http://web.archive.org/web/20030427162555/www.sage.edu/RSC/programs/globcomm/division/students/hendricks.html> (May 21, 2007).

6. Foster Hailey, "4 Negroes Jailed in Birmingham As the Integration Drive Slows," *The New York Times*, April 5, 1963, p. 16.
7. Ibid.
8. Andrew M. Manis, *A Fire You Can't Put Out: The Civil Rights Life of Birmingham's Fred Shuttlesworth* (Tuscaloosa, Ala.: The University of Alabama Press, 1999), p. 350.
9. Martin Luther King, Jr., *Why We Can't Wait* (New York: Signet Books, 2000), p. 63.
10. David L. Lewis, *King: A Critical Biography* (Baltimore: Penguin Books, Inc., 1970), p. 180.
11. Glenn T. Eskew, *But for Birmingham: The Local and National Movements in the Civil Rights Struggle* (Chapel Hill, N.C.: University of North Carolina Press, 1997), p. 225.
12. Foster Hailey, "Police Break up Alabama March," *The New York Times*, April 8, 1963, p. 31.
13. Foster Hailey, "Negroes Uniting in Birmingham," *The New York Times*, April 11, 1963, p. 21.
14. Andrew Young, *An Easy Burden: The Civil Rights Movement and the Transformation of America* (New York: HarperCollins, 1996), p. 205.
15. Taylor Branch, *Parting the Waters: America in the King Years, 1954–63* (New York: Simon and Schuster, 1988), p. 711.

CHAPTER 4. The Arrest of Dr. King

1. Martin Luther King, Jr., "Letter From Birmingham Jail," *The King Center* <http://www.thekingcenter.org/prog/non/Letter.pdf> (June 2007).
2. Foster Hailey, "Negroes Defying Birmingham Writ," *The New York Times*, April 12, 1963, p. 13.
3. Taylor Branch, *Parting the Waters: America in the King Years, 1954–1963* (New York: Simon and Schuster, 1988), p. 727.
4. Diane McWhorter, *Carry Me Home: Birmingham, Alabama: The Climactic Battle of the Civil Rights Revolution* (New York: Touchstone, 2001), p. 341.
5. Glenn T. Eskew, *But for Birmingham: The Local and National Movements in the Civil Rights Struggle* (Chapel Hill, N.C.: University of North Carolina Press, 1997), p. 239.

6. Howell Raines, *My Soul is Rested: The Story of the Civil Rights Movement in the Deep South* (New York: G. P. Putnam's Sons, 1977), p. 143.
7. Andrew Young, *An Easy Burden: The Civil Rights Movement and the Transformation of America* (New York: HarperCollins, 1996), p. 214.
8. King, p. 72.
9. Ralph Abernathy, *And the Walls Came Tumbling Down: An Autobiography* (New York: Harper & Row, 1989), p. 249.
10. Martin Luther King, Jr., *Why We Can't Wait* (New York: Signet Books, 2000), pp. 59–60.
11. Abernathy, p. 251.
12. Ibid.
13. Young, p. 216.
14. Ibid., pp. 220–221.
15. King, pp. 61–62.
16. McWhorter, p. 347.
17. "Statement by Alabama Clergymen," *The Martin Luther King, Jr., Research and Education Institute.* n.d., <http://www.stanford.edu/group/King/popular_requests/frequentdocs/clergy.pdf> (October 10, 2006).
18. King, "Letter from Birmingham Jail."
19. Ibid.
20. Ibid.
21. Ibid.
22. Ibid
23. Ibid.
24. Ibid.
25. Ibid.
26. David J. Garrow, *Bearing the Cross: Martin Luther King, Jr., and the Southern Christian Leadership Conference* (New York: Quill, 1986), p. 247.
27. Foster Hailey, "Dr. King Leaves Birmingham Jail," *The New York Times,* April 21, 1963, p. 70.

CHAPTER 5. The Children March

1. Diane McWhorter, *Carry Me Home: Birmingham, Alabama: The Climactic Battle of the Civil Rights Revolution* (New York: Touchstone, 2001), p. 366.

2. Taylor Branch, *Parting the Waters: America in the King Years, 1954–1963* (New York: Simon and Schuster, 1988), pp. 734–735.
3. Branch, p. 735.
4. Henry Hampton and Steve Fayer, *Voices of Freedom: An Oral History of the Civil Rights Movement from the 1950s through the 1980s* (New York: Bantam Books, 1990.), p. 132.
5. Ibid., p. 131.
6. Ibid., p. 132.
7. Sanford Wexler. *The Civil Rights Movement: An Eyewitness History* (New York: Facts on File, 1993), p. 172.
8. Andrew Young, *An Easy Burden: The Civil Rights Movement and the Transformation of America* (New York: HarperCollins, 1996), p. 236.
9. Ibid.
10. McWhorter, p. 361.
11. Andrew M. Manis, *A Fire You Can't Put Out: The Civil Rights Life of Birmingham's Fred Shuttlesworth* (Tuscaloosa, Ala.: The University of Alabama Press, 1999), p. 368.
12. "Robert Kennedy Warns of 'Increasing Turmoil,'" *The New York Times*, May 4, 1963, p. 8.
13. McWhorter, p. 363.
14. Ibid., p. 365.
15. Ibid., p. 366.
16. Glenn T. Eskew, "The Alabama Christian Movement for Human Rights," in David J. Garrow, Jr., ed., *Birmingham Alabama, 1956–1963: The Black Struggle for Civil Rights* (Brooklyn, New York: Carson Publishing, Inc., 1989), p. 82.
17. Ellen Levine, *Freedom's Children: Young Civil Rights Activists Tell Their Own Stories* (New York: Puffin Books, 2000), pp. 78–79.
18. Foster Hailey, "500 Are Arrested in Negro Protest at Birmingham," *The New York Times*, May 3, 1963, p. 1.
19. Ibid.
20. Ibid.
21. McWhorter, p. 368.
22. Ibid.
23. Ibid.

CHAPTER 6. "Fire Hoses on Those Black Girls"

1. Henry Hampton and Steve Fayer, *Voices of Freedom: An Oral History of the Civil Rights Movement from the 1950s through the 1980s* (New York: Bantam Books, 1990), p. 133.
2. Glenn T. Eskew, *But for Birmingham: The Local and National Movements in the Civil Rights Struggle* (Chapel Hill, N.C.: University of North Carolina Press, 1997), p. 265.
3. Diane McWhorter, *Carry Me Home: Birmingham, Alabama: The Climactic Battle of the Civil Rights Revolution* (New York: Touchstone, 2001), p. 368.
4. Ellen Levine, *Freedom's Children: Young Civil Rights Activists Tell Their Own Stories* (New York: Puffin Books, 2000), p. 85.
5. Eskew, p. 266.
6. Foster Hailey, "Dogs and Hoses Repulse Negroes at Birmingham," *The New York Times*, May 4, 1963, p. 8.
7. McWhorter, p. 371.
8. Ibid.
9. Levine, p. 85.
10. Hailey, p. 8.
11. "Birmingham Jail Is So Crowded Breakfast Takes Four Hours," *The New York Times,* May 8, 1963, p. 29.
12. Ibid.
13. Levine, p. 79.
14. Ibid., pp. 80–81.
15. Eskew, p. 266.
16. M. S. Handler, "Malcolm X Terms Dr. King's Tactics Futile," *The New York Times,* May 11, 1963, p. 9.
17. Hampton and Fayer, p. 133.
18. W. Stuart Towns, *We Want our Freedom: Rhetoric of the Civil Rights Movement* (Westport, Conn.: Praeger Publishers, 2002), p. 147.
19. Taylor Branch, *Parting the Waters: America in the King Years, 1954–1963* (New York: Simon and Schuster, 1988), p. 763.
20. Towns, pp. 150–151.
21. Ibid., pp. 148–151.
22. "Tape Reveals JFK's Frustration with Civil Rights Progress," *John F. Kennedy Library Newsletter,* March 6, 2005, <http://www.cs.umb.

edu/~rwhealan/jfk/newsletter_winter-spring2005_05.html>
(October 14, 2006).

23. Victor Navasky, *Kennedy Justice* (New York: Atheneum, 1971), p. 177.

24. Foster Hailey, "Birmingham Talks Pushed; Negroes March Peacefully," *The New York Times*, May 6, 1963, p. 59.

25. Foster Hailey, "U.S. Seeking a Truce in Birmingham; Hoses Again Drive Off Demonstrators," *The New York Times*, May 5, 1963, p. 82.

26. Lee E. Bains, Jr., "Birmingham, 1963: Confrontation over Civil Rights," in David J Garrow, Jr., ed., *Birmingham Alabama, 1956–1963: The Black Struggle for Civil Rights* (Brooklyn, New York: Carson Publishing, Inc., 1989), p. 271.

27. McWhorter, p. 378.

28. Hampton and Fayer, pp. 134–135.

29. Foster Hailey, "U.S. Seeking Truce in Birmingham; Hoses Again Drive off Demonstrators," *The New York Times*, May 5, 1963, p. 2.

30. McWhorter, p. 386.

31. Foster Hailey, "Birmingham Talks Pushed; Negroes March Peacefully," *The New York Times*, May 6, 1963, p. 1.

32. Levine, p. 88.

33. McWhorter, p. 387.

34. Ibid.

CHAPTER 7. The Children March On

1. "Birmingham, Alabama, 1963: Mass Meeting," *Folkways Record 5487*, recording of May 6, 1963 mass meeting.

2. Claude Sitton "Birmingham Jails 1,000 More Negroes," *The New York Times*, May 7, 1963, p. 33.

3. Ibid.

4. Diane McWhorter, *Carry Me Home: Birmingham, Alabama: The Climactic Battle of the Civil Rights Revolution* (New York: Touchstone, 2001), p. 390.

5. Sitton, p. 33.

6. Dick Gregory, *Nigger: An Autobiography* (New York: E. P. Dutton & Company, Inc., 1964), p. 178.

7. Sitton, p. 33.

8. Ibid.

9. Ibid.

10. Ibid.
11. Ibid., p. 1.
12. Ibid.
13. Taylor Branch, *Parting the Waters: America in the King Years, 1954–1963* (New York: Simon and Schuster, 1988), p. 771.
14. Sitton, p. 33.
15. "Birmingham, Alabama, 1963: Mass Meeting."
16. Ibid.
17. Andrew Young, *An Easy Burden: The Civil Rights Movement and the Transformation of America* (New York: HarperCollins, 1996), p. 242.
18. Claude Sitton "Rioting Negroes Routed by Police at Birmingham," *The New York Times*, May 8, 1963, p. 28.
19. "The 1963 Inaugural Address of George C. Wallace," *Alabama Department of Archives and History*, April 12, 2002, <http://www.archives.state.al.us/govs_list/inauguralspeech.html> (October 21, 2006).
20. Sitton, "Rioting Negroes Routed by Police at Birmingham," p. 28.
21. Ibid.
22. Ibid., p. 1.
23. Ibid.
24. McWhorter, p. 397.
25. Len Holt, "Eyewitness: The Police Terror at Birmingham," in *Reporting Civil Rights, Part One: American Journalism 1941–1963* (New York: The Library of America, 2003), p. 798.
26. Branch, 776.
27. Martin Luther King, Jr., *Why We Can't Wait* (New York: Signet Books, 2000), pp. 93–94.
28. Sitton, "Rioting Negroes Routed by Police at Birmingham," p. 1.
29. Holt, p. 799.
30. McWhorter, p. 404.
31. Sitton "Rioting Negroes Routed by Police at Birmingham," p. 28.
32. Fred L. Shuttlesworth, "Birmingham Revisited: Minister Returns to City to View Decade of Change," *Ebony*, August 1971, p. 118.
33. Ibid.
34. Sitton, "Rioting Negroes Routed by Police at Birmingham," p. 28.

CHAPTER 8. A Settlement Is Reached

1. "Negro Leaders' Statement on Birmingham Accord," *The New York Times*, May 11, 1963, p. 8.

2. Diane McWhorter, *Carry Me Home: Birmingham, Alabama: The Climactic Battle of the Civil Rights Revolution* (New York: Touchstone, 2001), p. 398.

3. Taylor Branch, *Parting the Waters: America in the King Years, 1954–1963* (New York: Simon and Schuster, 1988), p. 780.

4. John D. Pomfret, "President Voices Birmingham Hope," *The New York Times*, May 8, 1963, p. 1.

5. Claude Sitton "Peace Talks Gain at Birmingham in a Day of Truce," *The New York Times*, May 9, 1963, p. 17.

6. David J. Garrow, *Bearing the Cross: Martin Luther King, Jr., and the Southern Christian Leadership Conference* (New York: Quill, 1986), pp. 256–257.

7. Howell Raines, *My Soul is Rested: The Story of the Civil Rights Movement in the Deep South* (New York: G. P. Putnam's Sons, 1977), p. 159.

8. Branch, p. 782.

9. "News Conference 55," *John F. Kennedy Presidential Library & Museum*, May 8, 1963, <http://www.jfklibrary.org/Historical+Resources/Archives/Reference+Desk/Press+Conferences/003POF05Pressconference55_05081963.htm> (October 21, 2006).

10. "Gov. Wallace's Statement," *The New York Times*, May 9, 1963, p. 17.

11. McWhorter, p. 421.

12. Claude Sitton "Birmingham Talks Reach an Accord on Ending Crisis," *The New York Times*, May 10, 1963, p. 14.

13. "Negro Leaders' Statements on Birmingham Accord," *The New York Times*, May 11, 1963, p. 8.

14. Glenn T. Eskew, "The Alabama Christian Movement for Human Rights," in David J. Garrow, Jr., ed., *Birmingham Alabama, 1956–1963: The Black Struggle for Civil Rights* (Brooklyn, New York: Carson Publishing, Inc., 1989), p. 89.

15. Claude Sitton, "Birmingham Pact Sets Timetable for Integration," *The New York Times*, May 11, 1963, p. 8.

16. "Dr. King's Statement," *The New York Times*, May 11, 1963, p. 8.

17. Ibid.
18. Andrew M. Manis, *A Fire You Can't Put Out: The Civil Rights Life of Birmingham's Fred Shuttlesworth* (Tuscaloosa, Ala.: The University of Alabama Press, 1999), p. 388.
19. Michael Dorman, *We Shall Overcome: A Reporter's Eyewitness Account of the Year of Racial Strife and Triumph* (New York: Dial Press, 1964), p. 165.
20. Eskew, p. 295.
21. Claude Sitton, "Birmingham Pact Sets Timetable for Integration," p. 8.
22. Dorman, p. 166.

CHAPTER 9. Violence and More Violence

1. "Kennedy Statement," *The New York Times*, May 13, 1963, p. 25.
2. "Freedom Now! Birmingham, Alabama, 1963," *Pacifica Radio Archive*, March 24, 2005, <http://www.crmvet.org/info/bham63.htm> (October 21, 2006).
3. Taylor Branch, *Parting the Waters: America in the King Years, 1954–1963* (New York: Simon and Schuster, 1988), p. 792.
4. Diane McWhorter, *Carry Me Home: Birmingham, Alabama: The Climactic Battle of the Civil Rights Revolution* (New York: Touchstone, 2001), p. 425.
5. Branch, p. 793.
6. Ibid.
7. "Freedom Now! Birmingham, Alabama, 1963."
8. "Explosion in Alabama," *Newsweek*, May 20, 1963, p. 26.
9. Claude Sitton, "50 Hurt in Negro Rioting After Birmingham Blasts," *The New York Times*, May 13, 1963, p. 24.
10. McWhorter, p. 429.
11. Sitton, p. 24.
12. "Freedom Now! Birmingham, Alabama, 1963."
13. Sitton, p. 24.
14. Howell Raines, *My Soul is Rested: The Story of the Civil Rights Movement in the Deep South* (New York: G. P. Putnam's Sons, 1977), p. 177.
15. Sitton, p. 24.
16. Branch, p. 295.

17. Ibid., p. 24.
18. Branch, p. 794.
19. Ibid., p. 795.
20. "Explosion in Alabama," p. 26.
21. "Chief Alabama Trooper: Albert Jennings Lingo," *The New York Times*, May 13, 1963, p. 25.
22. Sitton, p. 24.
23. "Explosion in Alabama," p. 26.
24. Jonathan Rosenberg and Zachary Karabell, *Kennedy, Johnson, and the Quest for Justice: The Civil Rights Tapes* (New York: W. W. Norton & Company, 2003), p. 101.
25. "Kennedy Statement," p. 25.
26. McWhorter, p. 440.
27. Sitton, p. 24.
28. "Telegram from Governor George Wallace of Alabama to President Kennedy," *American Experience, 2002–2003*, <http://www.pbs.org/wgbh/amex/presidents/35_kennedy/psources/ps_wallgram.html> (October 21, 2006).
29. "Statement by Wallace and Boutwell," *The New York Times*, May 13, 1963, p. 24.
30. Michael Dorman, *We Shall Overcome: A Reporter's Eyewitness Account of the Year of Racial Strife and Triumph* (New York: Dial Press, 1964), p. 175.
31. "Freedom Now! Birmingham, Alabama, 1963."
32. Dorman, p. 205.
33. Ibid.
34. Branch, p. 801.
35. Ibid., pp. 801–802.

CHAPTER 10. "Don't Try to Stop Us"

1. Michael Dorman, *We Shall Overcome: A Reporter's Eyewitness Account of the Year of Racial Strife and Triumph* (New York: Dial Press, 1964), p. 213.
2. Dorman, p. 212.
3. Ibid., p. 213.

4. Cliff MacKay, "Police Dogs in Ala. Spur N.C. Unrest," in *Reporting Civil Rights, Part One: American Journalism 1941–1963* (New York: The Library of America, 2003), p. 820.

5. The Associated Press, "Greensboro Protests Go On; Mass Arrests are Resumed," *The New York Times*, June 7, 1963, p. 14.

6. Ibid.

7. The Associated Press, "400 Demonstrate in Savannah, GA," *The New York Times*, June 19, 1963, p. 22.

8. The Associated Press, "261 Held as Savannah Negroes March on Police Headquarters," *The New York Times*, June 20, 1963, p. 19.

9. R. Hart Phillips, "Tear Gas Routs Florida Negroes," *The New York Times*, May 31, 1963, p. 1.

10. Taylor Branch, *Parting the Waters: America in the King Years, 1954–1963* (New York: Simon and Schuster, 1988), p. 864.

11. Ibid., p. 825.

12. Diane McWhorter, *Carry Me Home: Birmingham, Alabama: The Climactic Battle of the Civil Rights Revolution* (New York: Touchstone, 2001), p. 447.

13. "Radio and Television Report to the American People on Civil Rights," June 11, 1963, *John F. Kennedy Presidential Library & Museum*, n.d. <http://www.jfklibrary.org/Historical+Resources/ Archives/Reference+Desk/Speeches/JFK/003POF03CivilRights 06111963.htm> (October 21, 2006).

14. Glenn T. Eskew, *But for Birmingham: The Local and National Movements in the Civil Rights Struggle* (Chapel Hill, N.C.: University of North Carolina Press, 1997), p. 317.

15. Harvard Sitkoff, *The Struggle for Black Equality* (New York: Hill and Wang, 1993), p. 149.

16. "'I Have a Dream' Address Delivered at the March on Washington for Jobs and Freedom," *The Martin Luther King, Jr., Research and Education Institute*, July 7, 2001, <http://www.stanford.edu/group/ King/publications/speeches/address_at_march_on_washington.pdf> (October 21, 2006).

17. E. W. Kenworthy, "200,000 March for Civil Rights in Orderly Washington Rally; President Sees Gain for Negroes," *The New York Times*, August 29, 1963, p. 16.

18. Herb Boyd, *We Shall Overcome* (Naperville, Illinois: Sourcebooks, Inc, 2004), p.162.

19. Ibid.

20. Claude Sitton, "Birmingham Bomb Kills 4 Negro Girls in Church; Riots Flare; 2 Boys Slain," *Reporting Civil Rights, Part Two: American Journalism 1963–1973* (New York: The Library of America, 2003), pp. 21–22.

21. Martin Luther King, Jr., "Eulogy for the Young Victims of the Sixteenth Street Baptist Church Bombing," September 18, 1963, *The Martin Luther King, Jr., Papers Project,* <http://www.stanford.edu/group/king/speeches/pub/Eulogy_For_the_martyred_children.html> (October 2007).

22. Charles and Barbara Whalen, *The Longest Debate: A Legislative History of the 1964 Civil Rights Act* (Washington, D.C.: Seven Locks Press, 1985), p. 79.

23. Eskew, p. 328.

24. Martin Luther King, Jr., "Letter From Birmingham Jail," *The King Center* <http://www.thekingcenter.org/prog/non/Letter.pdf> (June 2007).

25. "Birmingham, Alabama, 1963: Mass Meeting," *Folkways Record 5487*, recording of May 6, 1963, mass meeting.

attorney general—The chief legal advisor for a governor or for the president of the United States. The attorney general for the United States runs the Department of Justice and is a member of the president's cabinet.

boycott—A group or individual's refusal to buy goods from or even deal with a store or some other enterprise as a form of protest.

civil disobedience—A form of protest where laws are purposefully violated in order to change the law or some policy.

civil rights—The protections and privileges to which all citizens in a particular country are entitled.

injunction—A court or judge's order to someone or to a group to either stop some action or require some action.

integration—The opening of facilities such as schools, parks, hotels, and restaurants to all people where previously certain racial or ethnic groups were kept out.

Jim Crow—The name used to refer to the web of laws and customs that formally kept African Americans in a separate and unequal position.

Negro—Once used to refer to an African American, this term is now considered insulting.

the philosophy of nonviolence—The philosophy guiding many activists in the civil rights movement, especially those associated with Dr. Martin Luther King, Jr. Many taking part in protests signed an agreement stating that they would not strike back if they were hit. Leaders from the non-violent wing of the movement hoped that such behavior would transform opponents.

segregation—The separation of people based on race or ethnicity in schools, hotels, restaurants, residences, and elsewhere.

sit-in—A form of protest where people seat themselves and then refuse to leave until their demands are agreed to or they are forcefully removed. Civil rights activists frequently used this form of protest at segregated facilities such as lunch counters.

Books

Abernathy, Donzaleigh. *Partners to History: Martin Luther King, Jr., Ralph David Abernathy, and the Civil Rights Movement*. New York: Crown Publishers, 2003.

Durham, Michael S. *Powerful Days: The Civil Rights Photography of Charles Moore*. Tuscaloosa, Ala.: University of Alabama Press, 2002.

George, Charles, ed. *Living Through the Civil Rights Movement*. Detroit: Greenhaven Press, 2007.

Kasher, Steven. *The Civil Rights Movement: A Photographic History, 1954–68*. Abbeville Press, 2000.

Manheimer, Ann S. *Martin Luther King, Jr.: Dreaming of Equality*. Minneapolis: Carolrhoda Books, 2005.

McWhorter, Diane. *The Civil Rights Movement From 1954 to 1968*. New York: Scholastic, 2007.

Sikora, Frank. *Until Justice Rolls Down: The Birmingham Church Bombing Case*. Tuscaloosa, Ala.: University of Alabama Press, 2005.

Welch, Catherine A. *Children of the Civil Rights Era*. Minneapolis: Carolrhoda Books, 2001.

Internet Addresses

Birmingham Civil Rights Institute
<http://www.bcri.org/index.html>

The Martin Luther King, Jr., Research and Education Institute
<http://www.stanford.edu/group/King/index.htm>

National Civil Rights Museum
<http://www.civilrightsmuseum.org/default.asp>

A

Abernathy, Ralph, 41, 44–45, 46, 47, 96, 97, 115, 117
arrest, 47–48, 113
Alabama Christian Movement for Human Rights (ACMHR), 20, 22, 25, 27, 34
Albany, Georgia demonstrations, 29–30, 41

B

Baez, Joan, 97
Bevel, James, 59–60, 62–64, 65, 66, 67, 71, 79, 89–90, 93, 102, 105, 139
Birmingham, Alabama, 155, 156
bombings, 5–6, 125, 127–128, 129, 149–152
City Hall, 34, 38, 39, 66, 67, 86, 87
riots, 129, 131–135
segregation, 7–12, 20, 27, 32, 145, 155–156
Birmingham News, 51–52, 94
Birmingham police, 39, 47, 59, 67, 68, 73, 75, 96
dogs, 39, 48, 77, 81, 83, 85, 142
integration, 20–22
Boutwell, Albert, 33, 81, 98, 139, 145, 153

C

Citizens Affairs Committee (CAC), 145
civil disobedience, 55
Civil Rights Act of 1964, 144, 152–153

Clark, Jim, 99, 100, 131–132
Connor, Theophilus Eugene "Bull," 20–22, 23, 24, 27, 32–33, 34, 39, 43, 44, 47, 48, 51, 59, 62–63, 66, 73, 74, 75, 77, 81, 85, 86–87, 90–91, 96, 99–100, 101, 102, 105–107, 121, 124, 132, 139

E

Evans, G. V., 75, 77

F

fire hosing, 68, 75, 77, 79, 83, 87, 90, 91, 96, 105–106
Freedom Ride, 22–25

G

Gadson, Mary, 74, 77
Gardner, Ed, 9, 33, 45
Gaston, A. G., 64, 65, 72, 74, 81, 98, 113
Gaston Motel, 44, 45, 62, 97, 111, 117, 124, 127, 128, 129, 133, 137
Ghandi, Mohatma, 63
Greensboro, North Carolina, 22, 142
Gregory, Dick, 94, 95

H

Hanes, Art, 116–117
Hendricks, Audrey Faye, 67–68, 79–80
Holt, Len, 105–106

J

Jackson, Jesse, 142
Jackson, Mississippi protest, 141–142

Jenkins, William A., Jr., 43, 44–46
Jim Crow laws, 8–11, 15, 155
Johnson, Lyndon, 152–153
Johnson, R. C., 66, 94

K

Kelly Ingram Park, 38–39, 67–68,
    74, 77, 79, 80, 81, 83, 87, 96,
    100, 105–106, 111, 129
Kennedy, John F., 41, 51, 85, 110,
    111, 112, 113–114, 115, 119,
    121, 122, 133–135, 143–144,
    146, 149, 152
Kennedy, Robert, 41, 64, 65, 85,
    113
King, A. D., 125, 127, 129, 131,
    133
King, Coretta Scott, 33, 51
King, Martin Luther, Jr., 7, 8, 27,
    145
    arrest, 47–48, 51, 113
    in Birmingham, 29–33, 34,
        37–38, 41, 42, 57, 65–66, 71,
        73, 74, 79, 80, 81, 82, 83, 86,
        92, 94–95, 98, 102, 105, 112,
        113, 114, 115, 117, 119–121,
        124–125, 135, 136–138, 139,
        151–152
    "I Have a Dream" speech, 146,
        147
    injunction, 43–47
    "Letter from Birmingham Jail,"
        51–55, 155
Ku Klux Klan, 11, 12, 20, 21, 22,
    23, 34, 121, 123–124, 125, 134,
    145, 151

L

Lingo, Al, 129, 131, 132–133, 134

M

Malcolm X, 81
March on Washington, 145–147,
    149
Marshall, Burke, 85–86, 98,
    110–111, 133–134, 135,
    143–144, 152
Montgomery bus boycott, 22, 44, 63

N

National Association for the
    Advancement of Colored People
    (NAACP), 19–20, 139
New Pilgrim Baptist Church, 89, 97
nonviolence, 37–38, 62, 63, 65, 75,
    79, 87, 102, 129, 137

P

Parker High School, 66, 74, 93
Patterson, Floyd, 138
Peck, James, 24–25
Phillips High School,
    attack, 18–19, 20
    integration, 15, 17
Pitts, Lucius, 98, 111
Prichett, Laurie, 30, 124
Project C, 31–32, 34–35
    boycott, 31, 99, 139
    criticism, 81–83
    first children's march, 66–68, 71
    marching, 37, 38–39, 45–48
    march on Monday, May 6,
        93–94, 96, 98–99, 102
    miracle march, 89–91

national attention, 83, 85–86, 133–135, 138

negotiation, 98–99, 109–113, 115–117, 119–121

second children's march, 74–75, 77, 79

sit-ins, 34, 38, 41

third children's march, 83, 86–87, 89

Tuesday march, 102–103, 105–107

Project X. *See* Project C.

R

Roberson, James, 5, 9, 11

Robinson, Jackie, 138, 139

Russell, Larry, 9, 11

S

Savannah, Georgia protest, 142–143

Senior Citizens Committee, 109, 116–117, 133, 135

Shelton, Bobby, 124

Shores, Arthur, 86

Shuttlesworth, Carolyn, 7, 17

Shuttlesworth, Fred, 4, 14, 28, 98, 145

    assassination attempt on, 5, 7, 8, 12–13, 15

    assault at school, 18–19

    civil rights movement, 7, 12, 15, 16–17, 19–20, 21, 22, 25, 27, 29, 30, 31, 33, 37, 38, 39, 65, 67, 71, 105, 106–107, 111–112, 113, 117, 119, 120, 129, 153

Shuttlesworth, Ricky, 7, 17, 18

Shuttlesworth, Ruby, 5, 7, 17, 18–19, 20

Sixteenth Street Baptist Church, 48, 59, 67, 74, 82, 87, 93, 97, 102, 105, 106, 111, 129, 149–152

Smyer, Sidney, 98, 109, 120–121, 133, 135, 145

Southern Christian Leadership Conference (SCLC), 27, 30–32, 33, 41, 44, 45, 51, 53, 60, 62, 82, 86, 97, 102, 106, 110, 131, 133, 137

Stewart, Shelly "The Playboy," 58, 62, 66, 74

Student Nonviolent Coordinating Committee (SNCC), 30, 101–102

T

Tarver, Judy, 80–81

U

U.S. Supreme Court, 25, 153

V

Vann, David, 81–82, 83, 98, 145

Voting Rights Act of 1965, 153, 155

W

Walker, Wyatt Tee, 31–32, 51, 57, 60, 86, 87, 89, 90, 127, 129, 131

Wallace, George, 99, 100–102, 105, 110, 114–115, 121, 132, 134, 135–136

"We Shall Overcome," 39, 47, 137

Y

Young, Andrew, 46, 47, 63, 65, 82, 98, 99, 112